T5-DHH-859

This book
belongs to

....

To Sam

FREDERICK WARNE

Published by the Penguin Group
Penguin Books Ltd, 80 Strand, London WC2R 0RL, England
Penguin Young Readers Group, 345 Hudson Street,
New York, New York 10014, U.S.A.
Penguin Books Australia Ltd, 250 Camberwell Road, Camberwell,
Victoria 3124, Australia
Canada, India, New Zealand, South Africa

7

Copyright © Frederick Warne & Co., 2006

New reproductions of Cicely Mary Barker's illustrations
copyright © The Estate of Cicely Mary Barker, 1990
Original text and illustrations copyright
© The Estate of Cicely Mary Barker,
1923, 1925, 1926, 1934, 1940, 1944, 1948

All rights reserved

Printed in Great Britain

Zinnia's Magical Adventure

by Pippa Le Quesne

Welcome to the Flower Fairy Garden!

Where are the fairies?
Where can we find them?
We've seen the fairy-rings
They leave behind them!

Is it a secret
No one is telling?
Why, in your garden
Surely they're dwelling!

No need for journeying,
Seeking afar:
Where there are flowers,
There fairies are!

Contents

Chapter One
Babysitting

"Yes, Your Majesty, I agree. Daisy does make quite the best fairy nectar in the garden," Zinnia said, lifting her bluebell cup and pretending to take a dainty sip.

Daisy giggled as she got to her feet, gathering the petals of her skirt in either hand. "Show me how you curtsy again," she said, putting out a leg in front of her and wobbling as she tried to bob down without losing her balance.

"Watch out!" Double Daisy shouted.
"Or you'll land in the crab-apple jelly—and
imagine what the Queen of the Meadow
would think of that!"

The two young Flower Fairies burst out
laughing.

Zinnia smiled to herself. Her little cousins
were very sweet and she loved spending time
with them, but it had been a long morning
since Daisy had come up with the idea of
a make-believe royal tea party. Zinnia had
made special daisy-chain garlands for each
of them and patiently tried to teach them
how they should bow and curtsy in front of

a queen. Double Daisy would lean so far forward that the red petals from his bonnet kept flopping in his eyes, causing him to topple over, and he and his sister to fall down laughing. And, of course, no matter how many times he did it, the funnier the two of them found it.

It had been very funny at first and Zinnia had been happy to have imaginary conversations with their regal guest, but now she was getting a bit bored of the game and longed to stretch her legs.

She couldn't help wondering what Beechnut and Hazelnut were up to. These adventurous fairies were always bursting with energy and up for a game of tag. The trouble was that they lived in the lane outside the garden boundaries. And Daisy and Double Daisy were too little to stray far from their flowers and too young to be left on their own.

Now they were concentrating hard on carrying bark plates piled high with imaginary food, supposedly presenting them to their guest. They were also arguing about whether the Queen of the Meadow would have arrived in a chariot pulled by dragonflies or if she would have flown in from the marshes on the back of a bird.

Zinnia sighed. It had been ages since she had been out of the garden, and it suddenly struck her that she must have been missing out on all sorts of excitement. Beechnut and Hazelnut got to see everything from their vantage point in the trees and they were always full of interesting stories—for one thing, lots of different humans used the lane to go about their daily business. Zinnia often spent time imagining what it would be like to live somewhere less predictable than the garden.

"You're daydreaming again!" a voice from above interrupted her thoughts.

Zinnia looked up. A Flower Fairy with rosy cheeks and pretty pink wings was sitting on the bough of the apple tree, swinging her legs.

"Apple Blossom!"

Zinnia was very pleased to see her friend. She was always cheerful and never got tired of playing with the younger

Flower Fairies.

"I was just thinking it might be nice to see what's going on in the lane this afternoon…" Zinnia paused. She suddenly had an idea. "Um… but of course I'm looking after my cousins," she went on, "and I would ask Sweet Pea, but she's busy teaching the baby fairies to climb—"

"I'd love to look after Daisy and Double Daisy," Apple Blossom interrupted. "Off you go, and have an adventure!" She began nimbly swinging from branch to branch until she was perched on the tip of the one nearest to the ground.

"Oh, you're wonderful!" Zinnia beamed as Apple Blossom flew down and landed on the grass.

The Tree Fairy gathered up Daisy in an enormous hug and then swung Double Daisy round and round by his arms.

"What are you up to, my lovelies?"

"We're having tea with the Queen of
the Meadow, of course," the two Daisies
chorused.

"Well, good afternoon, Your Highness,
what an honor," Apple Blossom said,
winking at Zinnia and curtsying very low
to the space between the two young Flower
Fairies.

Zinnia waved good bye and blew a kiss to
her cousins. They would have a great time

with Apple Blossom, and she'd be back long before their bedtime. As she headed for the wall at the bottom of the garden, there was a definite spring to her step, and she felt a sudden surge of excitement. She had the whole afternoon to herself, and who knew what lay ahead of her?

"Horse Chestnut! Where are you?" Zinnia called, parting the large green leaves of his tree to peer up among the higher branches. She had made light work of the garden wall, which was old stone and had plenty of footholds, and, after a quick look up and down the lane to check it was safe, she had flown straight for her friend's tree.

"Horse Chestnut, are you there?"

Zinnia ran lightly along the length of the branch until she was right inside the canopy of leaves, where she leaned against the trunk of the tree to catch her breath. She tucked a loose strand of hair behind her ear and straightened the daisy garland on her head, expecting Horse Chestnut's mischievous face to appear at any moment.

Mind you, she thought, *it would be more like him to come whizzing out of nowhere and surprise me!*

Horse Chestnut always dressed entirely in green and brown, including his green spiky helmet, so he was quite difficult to spot and was an expert at sudden appearances.

"Today I will be ready for him," Zinnia said resolutely, thinking aloud. She listened intently for any sign of movement but could only hear the distant song of a blackbird and the leaves of the tree stirring gently in the breeze.

After a few moments without any sign of Horse Chestnut,

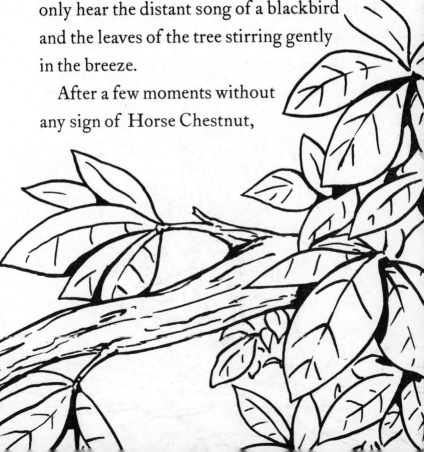

Zinnia began to relax. She watched a field mouse dart across the dusty lane and scurry into a hedgerow, and she wondered if Horse Chestnut had gone to visit Beechnut. She would go and look for both of them in a minute, she decided, but for now she was enjoying her view of the world from above. Being high up made her aware that she was out in a much larger open space than usual,

and compared to the garden, with its familiar beds and borders, it seemed to brim with possibilities.

At that moment, Zinnia's thoughts were interrupted by the sound of excited chatter followed by a loud laugh. It seemed to be coming from farther up the lane. And if she wasn't mistaken, it was the sound of *human* children heading toward her!

Taking care to be as quiet as she could, Zinnia crept along the branch to get a better view. Luckily there was a particularly large horse chestnut leaf for her to hide behind, and, flattening her wings against her back, she made sure that none of the bright pink petals of her skirt were poking out.

You see, Flower Fairies can see humans, and they know all about them. They are even allowed to help humans, but on no account are they ever to let humans catch sight of them. When Zinnia had officially been given her flower and become a proper Flower Fairy, wise Wild Rose had explained to her that generally humans were very friendly. However, they were also curious beings —especially children—and if they knew that there really were fairies living in their world and even in their own gardens, they would never leave them alone, and it would be impossible for the Flower Fairy Garden to continue its peaceful existence.

Zinnia took a deep breath and bravely popped her head out from behind the leaf. She had seen the humans that lived in the house at the top of the garden on numerous occasions, but the insects feel the vibrations in the grass first and would always give the fairies ample warning. This time Zinnia was unprepared and she was alone.

The children were nearly below the tree now. A boy and a girl with dark hair and very similar features were hurrying along at quite a pace, and a smaller girl with flushed red cheeks was struggling to keep up with them.

"Come on, Emily, you're such a slowpoke!" the boy called to her.

"Shut up, Tom," she replied, puffing. "If it wasn't for me you'd still be complaining about how boring playing in the garden is."

"And she was the last one to climb over the gate," his twin sister reminded him. "Anyway, because it was Emily's idea to explore the

marsh she should lead the way."

"Who made you expedition organizer, Charlotte?" Tom said, but Zinnia could see that he had a grin on his face, and he'd slowed down so that his younger sister could catch up.

"Will there be quicksand? Who do you think we'll meet on the marsh? Do wild animals live there?" Emily chirped away, too busy asking questions to wait for the answers.

Zinnia watched them disappearing down the lane, not moving a muscle for several moments. The Flower Fairy wasn't fixed to the spot because she was afraid they'd catch sight of her—they had been so absorbed in their conversation that they hadn't even looked up once—but because she'd had a brainstorm. She'd never been to the marsh, and she'd certainly never met any of the Wild Flower Fairies that lived there. Their very name suggested that they must be far more exotic than any of the fairies Zinnia knew. That was it! Forget playing tag in the lane— she was off for a real adventure.

"Show me the way!" she called boldly after the retreating figures, knowing that her voice was too tiny for them to hear at a distance. With that, she took a joyous leap into the air and beat her wings as fast as she could in order to follow the children.

Chapter Three
Time to Explore

"You're it!"

Charlotte shrieked with glee as she tagged her brother. She turned on her heel, her shoes squelching along the boggy path as she ran.

"Mom's going to kill us!" Emily giggled as she dived into the long rush-grass, just managing to escape Tom's grasp.

The marsh was like nowhere Zinnia had ever been before.

The children had climbed over a stile that led directly from the lane on to the marsh, and she had done her best to keep up with them as they splashed along the waterlogged path that cut across it. They whooped and called to one another, flitting in and out of the tall grasses that seemed more like a forest to the Flower Fairy than the short, spiky grass that neatly bordered the flower bed where she lived.

When finally the children had taken a break from their game to catch their breath, Zinnia landed on a grass with dense and cottony heads. It provided her with a comfortable resting place. The marshland seemed to stretch as far as she could see in every direction—

a sea of grass that met the horizon, the muted green unbroken by any of the bright flowers or blossom trees that she was accustomed to.

In comparison, the fuchsia pink of her skirt looked even more dazzling than usual, and so she had to be doubly careful not to let the children spot her.

At first, Zinnia had flown behind them at a safe distance, but soon she became bolder, and it wasn't long before she was so close that if they'd turned their heads she wouldn't have more than a split second to hide.

And then it became a game of dare—weaving
in and out of the grasses after the children, or
darting on to the path and flying right behind
them before plunging back amidst the stalks
at the last moment.

Phew! she thought to herself as she sank back into the fluffy cushions. *Apple Blossom and the Daisies will never believe how far I've flown today.* She smiled to herself, imagining their surprise.

Garden Flower Fairies don't fly long distances—they walk as much as they can and tend to take to the air to get up into the trees or just for fun. If they have farther to go they hitch a lift with a friendly bird or dragonfly. Zinnia was just picturing her friends' faces as she told them all about the children and following them to the marsh, when a flash of purple caught her eye. She felt a rush of adrenaline. Could it be one of the Wild Flower Fairies that she'd come to meet? Tingling with anticipation, she launched herself into the air to find out.

When she landed she headed in the
direction she thought the fairy had taken.
And sure enough—just beyond the path,
behind a clump of rush-grass—sat not just
one Flower Fairy, but three!

The fairy that Zinnia had seen sat with her
knees pulled up to her chin, a torn green
smock all but covering her purple-petal
dress, and her long brown hair pulled back in
two messy plaits. She had beautiful purple-

and-white wings, but Zinnia was shocked to
see how dusty they looked—she had never
come across a Flower Fairy that seemed to
care less about her appearance! Cross-legged
in front of her were two boy fairies—both
with pointed ears, plain white wings, and,
Zinnia noticed, clothes the color of the
surrounding grasses. In fact, one of them
had tufty blond hair like the flower head that
she'd sat on, and the other wore a grass girdle
around his tunic that was hemmed with small
brown seeds.

"Er, hello," she ventured, feeling quite
nervous as she stepped out into the clearing.

"Wow, look at you!" the female Flower
Fairy burst out, jumping to her feet. "I've
never seen such magnificent wings."

"They're the same as the painted lady
butterflies," Zinnia said timidly. "And my
skirt is from my flower—Zinnia," she added,

quite taken aback by the confident fairy
who was walking slowly around her, openly
admiring her clothes.

"I'm Mallow, but most people call me
Rags-and-Tatters on account of the state of
me!" Mallow laughed warmly, and Zinnia
couldn't help but like her immediately.

"And I'm Cotton-Grass and this is my
brother Rush-Grass," the blond boy fairy
said, pointing to his companion,
whose face broke into a
broad grin.

"Come and join
us—we've been
spying on some
newcomers,"
said Mallow,
cocking her
head in the
direction of

the sound of the children's chatter. She sat down and patted the ground next to her. "And you're certainly not from around here, looking as neat as a new pin!"

"I'm from the garden," Zinnia explained. "Quite a long way from here, actually," she went on, no longer feeling shy.

"Oh, the garden," Rush-Grass said. "Heard all about it, but never been myself."

"I've seen it once." Mallow nodded wisely. "Peeked over the wall on my travels. I sell my seeds as fairy cheeses at the market. Fairy housewives and elves can't get enough of them!" she explained, picking up from beside her what looked to Zinnia like a miniature pumpkin.

"That garden's very cozy-looking", said Cotton-Grass.

"Sounds a bit tame, if you ask me," Rush-Grass piped up, but not unkindly.

Zinnia wasn't sure if she liked her home being called cozy or tame. It was very ordered, and life was comfortable there, but she didn't want the marsh dwellers to think she was boring.

"Oh, but there's always plenty going on. And um, I don't really spend much time there—I'm always off exploring," she boasted uncertainly.

"Well, you should come and see the sights with us. Never a dull moment on the marsh. Every day's an adventure!" Cotton-Grass said enthusiastically. "And the best part is that we never know where we'll be at nightfall."

"What do you mean?" Zinnia asked, enthralled.

"Sleep where we end up—make do with whatever pillow we can find, of course!" Rush-Grass exclaimed, jumping to his feet and stretching his arms out wide.

"You should try it. Nothing beats sleeping out—with nothing between you and the stars. How about tonight?" Cotton-Grass offered.

Zinnia gulped. The thought of darkness drawing in without the comfort of her familiar flower or a moss blanket to pull over her wasn't very appealing—even if it was an adventure ... But on the other hand, she couldn't let her new friends think she was any less courageous than them. No—she would show them what a Garden Flower Fairy was made of!

Chapter Four
New Friends

Just then there was a low whistle from a
nearby clump of grass.

"Hey, Cotton, Rush—come here. I think
you're needed," whispered Mallow, who had
wandered off to keep an eye on the children.

Zinnia had been vaguely aware of the
absence of laughter and the tone of the
children's voices changing. And now, as she
peeked over Mallow's shoulder, it was
obvious that they were no longer
enjoying themselves.

They were quite a different sight from the
three children who had been in high spirits
earlier that afternoon. Aside from the messy
state of their clothes, they looked tired and
decidedly miserable.

"I'm starving," Tom complained, kicking
at a muddy puddle with the toe of his shoe.

"There's no use in saying that over and
over again," said Charlotte. "You know we've
missed snack time and we'll be lucky if Mom
doesn't send us to bed without anything to
eat."

"And we still haven't found my shoe," Emily wailed. She was in particularly bad shape—her plump little legs and feet were caked in mud, and and her skirt was covered in grass stains. Zinnia thought she looked quite comical, and it reminded her of her Daisy cousins, which in turn made her feel quite homesick.

"Seeing as you don't even know when it came off, we're never going to find it," Tom said grumpily. "And I don't know about you, but I have no idea what direction we came from."

Charlotte, who was frantically searching through the grass, looked up. "We just need to find the path, and then even if we go in the wrong direction at least we'll know the other way will take us back to the lane," she said, looking less sure than she sounded.

"That's our job," Rush-Grass whispered to Zinnia. "We help whoever's got lost on the marsh to find their way home."

"How do you do that without them seeing you though?" Zinnia asked.

"A little bit of fairy dust and a bit more speed," chortled Cotton-Grass, who was unfolding a large dock leaf that he had been carrying as a knapsack.

"People generally follow bright lights, even if it isn't dark—it makes them feel hopeful." Rush-Grass beamed at Zinnia. "So we just catch their eye with some fairy dust, make some noise, and then fly to the path as fast as we can." He took a handful of the fine powder.

"Perhaps you should go back with them," Mallow suggested. "It's time that I got myself ready for market tomorrow, so I'd better be off."

Zinnia was about to gratefully agree when she remembered their conversation about the garden and how she'd boasted about being adventurous. Although she wasn't sure she knew her way home, she felt confident that if she flew above the grass she'd get her bearings quickly enough. "Oh, don't worry about me," she said cheerily. "I've still got some exploring to do."

"Travel well, then," Cotton said, opening his wings.

"Farewell, ladies," said his brother. As he took off, he blew the fairy dust into the air. "Light up!" he commanded.

Zinnia watched the tiny particles glow to life and dance away on the breeze. "Good-bye!" she called as the Grass Fairies

followed.
"Well," said
Mallow, turning to the
Garden Fairy and taking
her hands, "it's been lovely to meet you, and
I hope it's not the last time." She turned to go
and then as an afterthought, held out a fat
mallow seed.

Zinnia took it gratefully and waved as
her friend disappeared through the tall
grass. "Maybe see you later?" she called after
her, as it suddenly struck her that she was
completely alone again.

"I'll eat the cheese and then I'll be on my way," Zinnia said, thinking aloud into the silence. It wasn't until she sat down that she realized how tired she was—all the excitement had kept her exhaustion at bay, but now her wings positively ached. "If only I'd brought some fairy dust with me."

Flower Fairies cannot cast spells as such, but ground-up pollen from each of their flowers gives them a little magic of their own. Walking all the way home seemed like an impossible task to Zinnia, but if she had some of her fairy dust she could have summoned the butterflies to accompany her.

Perhaps I am going to have to sleep here tonight, she thought as she took a bite of the cheese. The mallow seed was delicious and instantly comforting and somehow helped her forget about her butterfly friends: some of Mallow's magic. Zinnia smiled as her spirits lifted further, and she reminded herself that plenty of Wild Flower Fairies slept out on the marsh, so it couldn't be that frightening.

She was just thinking that Cotton-Grass and Rush-Grass might be back before too long when she was startled by a rustling in the grass behind her. She looked around, expecting to see an insect or a bird but there was no one.

There it was again—more rustling, but this time to the left of her, and it was followed by a stifled giggle.

"Rush? Cotton? Is that you?"

But there was no answer, just more rustling.

"Mallow?" Zinnia called optimistically, hoping that her friend had finished her work quickly and come back to find her.

The Garden Fairy got to her feet and shivered. The heat had gone out of the

afternoon sun, and for the first time she
noticed how much colder it was without the
shelter of the garden wall.

I may as well start heading home, she thought.
*Even if I don't find the path, at least moving will
warm me up.*

Hearing another giggle, Zinnia hurried
to pick up the remainder of the mallow seed.
But she was too late—the grasses parted and
two creatures dressed entirely in dark green
rushed out at her.

"Fairy cheese and a pretty
little fairy to go
with it!" said one
gleefully and the
other snatched
the seed from her
hands, causing
her to lose her
balance.

Zinnia looked up at the sly eyes staring back
at her; then she looked at the long pointed
ears and the hoods covering messy hair. And
finally she noticed not only the lack of shoes
but, more importantly, the pointed wings on
the back of the creatures.

"You're elves!" Zinnia gasped, and before she could stop herself, she burst into tears.

Chapter Five
Naughty Elves

"Crybaby! Crybaby!" chanted the elves, dancing round Zinnia in delight.

At first they had been stunned into silence by the Garden Fairy's outburst, but now that she had dried her eyes and was looking cross rather than sad, they had set about poking fun at her.

After shedding a few tears, Zinnia felt a lot better, and now the elves were infuriating her. Their energy seemed to be limitless, and no matter how many times she tried to dodge past one of them, the other would be there, barring her way. "Give me back my cheese and let me go!" she exclaimed, trying to grab the mallow seed from the nearest elf as he blocked her path.

But he threw it over her head to his companion, giggling almost uncontrollably.

"Can't give you the cheese—that's ours
for the eating," said the other elf, taking an
enormous bite and all but finishing it off.
"But you're free to go whenever you want.
Isn't she?" He winked at his friend and threw
him back the last of the mallow seed.

"Although that's not to say we won't follow
you, pretty one," mocked his mate, cramming
what was left into his mouth.

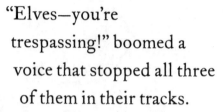

"Elves—you're trespassing!" boomed a voice that stopped all three of them in their tracks. The next moment into the clearing walked the most resplendent Flower Fairy Zinnia had ever seen. He was older than her with a distinguished air about him, but he had a youthful, handsome face. Apart from his leaf-green mantle and slippers, he was clothed from head to toe in shimmering gold, and on his head he wore a crown of bright yellow flower stamens.

"Kingcup!" breathed Zinnia, trembling a little as she curtseyed.

When she looked up, she saw that the king was smiling at her tenderly, and although this was the first time she had met him, she felt instantly at ease.

As for the elves, they were a pathetic sight, cowering before the regal Flower Fairy, unrecognizable as the two creatures that had been taunting Zinnia just moments before.

"You are trespassing on Flower Fairy territory." Kingcup turned to them. "And for stealing from one of my kind, you are banished from the marsh—now be gone!"

The elves scrambled to their feet. "Yes, Your Majesty, many apologies, Your Majesty," they mumbled as they fell over each other to escape from the clearing first.

When they had gone, the king turned back to Zinnia with a twinkle in his eye. "Well, I think they were suitably told off, don't you? They don't really mean any harm; they just can't resist fairy cheese." He chuckled and then added, "or teasing!"

Zinnia breathed a sigh of relief. "Thank you so much for rescuing me," she said gratefully. 'I realized fairly soon that they weren't dangerous—but they were maddening, and they wouldn't let me go."

"Presumably you mean home?" Kingcup

said, taking Zinnia by the hand and leading her out of the clearing. Soon they had found the path, and as they walked he asked her, "What are you doing so far from the garden so late in the day?"

Zinnia began relaying the events of the afternoon, feeling a little foolish when it came to the part about showing off to the Wild Flower Fairies, but the king just smiled as if it was a mistake he could have easily made himself.

"Well," said Kingcup when she had finished, "I'm assuming that you'd like to go back to the garden tonight?" He waited for Zinnia to nod in response. "Then you're in luck. A dear friend of mine that is visiting will be heading back your way, and I'm sure

she'd be more than glad to take you."

They'd left the path now and were picking their way across much wetter ground. Soon there were small pools of water, and it was not long before it was obvious to Zinnia that they had reached Kingcup's realm. Growing out of the pools were clusters of marsh marigolds with their kidney-shaped leaves and shiny golden flowers like giant buttercups. And sitting amongst them was a Flower Fairy with long blonde hair, delicate shell- pink wings and a tiara of rose stamens.

"Wild Rose!" Zinnia cried out happily.

"So, I see your stroll was rather eventful," Wild Rose remarked to Kingcup as she fluttered over to join them. She kissed the top of Zinnia's head and murmured, "Sweet Garden Fairy, what are you doing here?"

"She's been having a grand adventure on the marsh," the king replied in good humor. "And I'm sure she'll tell you all about it on your way home."

"Oh yes, of course." Wild Rose nodded wisely. Then, glancing at the weary Garden Fairy, she said, "I think we'll summon a moorhen and see if we can catch a ride home."

Zinnia was very pleased to hear that they wouldn't be making the journey on foot, as ever since she had been in the comforting presence of Wild Rose, waves of tiredness had begun to wash over her. She would have gladly slept in precisely the spot she was standing.

Once Kingcup had clapped his hands, they didn't have to wait for more than a few moments before a friendly looking bird with black glossy feathers and a vivid red-and-yellow beak landed in the water beside them. Without further ado, the king bade them farewell. "Goodbye, Rose, see you soon," he said, kissing her on both cheeks.

Zinnia watched Wild Rose mount the moorhen and sit elegantly with her legs and skirt to one side. Then she clambered up in front of her and wrapped her arms around the bird's neck in preparation for take-off.

"It was an honor to meet you, Your Majesty," she called to Kingcup. "Sorry you had to come and save me."

"It was a pleasure—and anyway, I didn't really save you. You were being very brave and the elves would have tired of their game soon enough. Now, off you go!"

* * *

"You know, I do enjoy living in the hedgerow and meeting all the Flower Fairies that pass by or come to visit me to be named. And I quite understand the lure of the unknown," said Wild Rose gently, "but you're very lucky to have a flower that resides out of harm's way. You always have a wonderful variety of company—so many different fairies to play with but all with familiar faces—as well as your own special butterfly friends."

Zinnia turned to say something in reply, but Wild Rose just raised a finger to her lips. "Look—here's the lane. We'll be there soon."

As they'd soared above the marsh, Zinnia had gazed down at the vast exposed area below, and she'd had a sense of just how small she was in comparison. Even with Wild Rose's arms encircling her waist, she'd suddenly felt quite lost, and as she listened to the words of the older Flower Fairy, she longed to be back in the garden. And there, far below them, but now in sight, was the garden. Zinnia's heart leaped at the sight of it and, with every ounce of her being, she willed the moorhen to fly faster.

Chapter Six
Bedtime Stories

"I didn't meet the Queen of the Meadow, but I did meet Kingcup!"

Zinnia was sitting on the edge of the moss blanket, under which Daisy and Double Daisy were snuggled, telling her two little cousins all about her adventure.

There had been great excitement when she had arrived on the back of the moorhen. It wasn't often that Wild Rose visited the garden, but she had a reputation as being the kindest and wisest of the Flower Fairies and was greatly loved by all who knew her. Zinnia had proudly introduced Wild Rose to Daisy and Double Daisy—who lost no time in informing her all about their royal tea party and showing her their very best curtsy and bow, which Apple Blossom had been helping them perfect.

"Can you stay until bedtime?" Double Daisy had begged, after insisting that she come and see the corner of the garden that he and Daisy lived in, where their starlike flowers were still lifting their faces to catch the last rays of sunshine.

"I've had a very long day out on the moor," replied Wild Rose, "and it's time I was getting home, but I promise to come back for one of your splendid tea parties. Besides, I have a feeling that someone has a particularly interesting bedtime story to tell you tonight,"

she added, looking directly at Zinnia.

When they had said their good-byes and the Daisies had stopped jumping around at the thought of entertaining Wild Rose, Zinnia finally managed to settle them down for the night. The two little Flower Fairies sat upright in their bed, their blanket pulled up to their chins, and listened with shining eyes as she told them all about following the children to the marsh and how she had met Cotton-Grass, Rush-Grass and Mallow. They asked her to repeat the bit about the elves three times before she could get to the part where Kingcup rescued her and took her to find Wild Rose.

"What was the best part of the day?" Daisy asked, rubbing her eyes sleepily.

"Coming home to you two," Zinnia said without hesitation, leaning over to kiss them both goodnight.

As the sun sank behind the garden wall and the last of the daisies closed its petals for the night, Zinnia sighed happily to herself. How could she ever get bored of the sight of her cousins sinking peacefully into sleep? She stood up and yawned. She couldn't imagine wanting to go off on an adventure for quite some time now, but the next time she did, it would be with the knowledge that the only place that she belonged at the end of the day was safely tucked up in her cozy corner of the garden.

FLOWER FAIRIES™ FRIENDS

Visit our Flower Fairies website at:

www.flowerfairies.com

There are lots of fun Flower Fairy games and
activities for you to play, plus you can find out more
about all your favorite fairy friends!

Have you logged onto the Flower Fairies™ Friends Friendship Ring?

In the land of Fairyopolis every fairy is your friend
and now the Flower Fairies
want to share their secrets with you!

Online Fun

No Membership Fee

Visit **www.flowerfairies.com**
and sign up for the Flower
Fairies Friendship Ring
and you will receive:

- ❀ Secret Fairy Coded Messages
- ❀ News and updates
- ❀ Invitations to special events
- ❀ Every new friend receives a
 special gift from the Flower Fairies!
 (while supplies last.)

Frederick Warne & Co.
A division of Penguin Young Readers Group

This book
belongs to

....

For Manda

FREDERICK WARNE

Published by the Penguin Group
Penguin Books Ltd, 80 Strand, London WC2R 0RL, England
Penguin Young Readers Group, 345 Hudson Street,
New York, New York 10014, U.S.A.
Penguin Books Australia Ltd, 250 Camberwell Road, Camberwell,
Victoria 3124, Australia
Canada, India, New Zealand, South Africa

3

Copyright © Frederick Warne & Co., 2006

New reproductions of Cicely Mary Barker's illustrations
copyright © The Estate of Cicely Mary Barker, 1990
Original text and illustrations copyright
© The Estate of Cicely Mary Barker,
1923, 1925, 1926, 1934, 1940, 1944, 1948

All rights reserved

Printed in Great Britain

Almond Blossom's Mystery

by Kay Woodward

Welcome to the Flower Fairy Garden!

Where are the fairies?
Where can we find them?
We've seen the fairy-rings
They leave behind them!

Is it a secret
No one is telling?
Why, in your garden
Surely they're dwelling!

No need for journeying,
Seeking afar:
Where there are flowers,
There fairies are!

Contents

Chapter One
The Longest Winter

None of the Flower Fairies could remember winter ever being *this* long. The bitterly cold weather seemed to have gone on for an eternity. It was months since they'd opened their presents beneath the decorated boughs of the Christmas tree, while the rusty colors of autumn were just a distant memory. It wouldn't have been so bad if the sun was shining, but that was missing too, hidden behind a thick layer of dull cloud.

At first the Flower Fairies, who are usually very optimistic creatures, were hopeful that spring was just around the corner. But when the cold, dreary weather continued, they became puzzled. Finally they began to worry. Would it be winter forever? Without the sun, how would their garden flourish? Would the buds and blossoms never appear? The fairies whispered in hushed voices to each other, desperate to learn the answer to the most important question of all: *Where was spring?*

There was one Flower Fairy in particular who was very concerned about the long winter, and that was Almond Blossom. Day after day, she peered up at the grim, gray sky and then looked closely at the bare branches of her tree.

"Nothing," she sighed. "Not even a bud." The pretty little fairy, no bigger than a human hand, slumped despondently against the tree trunk.

Spring was the most important event on Almond Blossom's calendar. Every year, as soon as winter

waved farewell,
the milder weather
encouraged her
delicate pink
blossoms to unfurl.
For all the other Flower
Fairies, this was the very first
sign of spring. For Almond Blossom,
it was her signal to perform the traditional
dance that heralded the new season. She so
enjoyed skipping and pirouetting around
the garden, brandishing one of her own
blossom-laden stems, to the sound of the
delighted cheers of the other fairies. It just
wouldn't be the same carrying a bare, brown
twig.

"Cheer up!" called Sycamore from his
lofty perch on a nearby tree. "Whatever
you're thinking about might never happen!"

"That's what I'm worried about," Almond

Blossom replied. "What if spring never happens— ever? What then?" Her pretty face crumpled and she sobbed great, fat tears of sorrow.

"What'll I do? I may as well just pack up my things and leave the Flower Fairies Garden!"

Sycamore looked utterly horrified at the effect his seemingly harmless greeting had had on poor Almond Blossom, and he leaped the short distance between their trees, his gauzy wings glowing gold and green in the pale light. "There, there," he said, patting her shoulder awkwardly. Sycamore was at his happiest when fluttering and twirling through the air, a little like the winged seeds that whirled from his tree every autumn— he didn't have much experience in making glum fairies laugh. But he did his best.

"Spring *will* come," he said gently. "Just you wait and see."

"That's very kind of you, Sycamore," said Almond Blossom, wiping away her

tears. She grabbed a dark green leaf and blew her nose into it noisily. "I don't know what's got into me. I think I might be missing the sun!" She laughed weakly.

Sycamore gave her an encouraging grin. "Soon it'll be so sunny that you'll wish for a cloud to come by to give you some shade!" he said.

But the dull, cloudy, cold weather continued. The only variation from the grayness was the occasional sharp shower that soaked and chilled any Flower Fairy unlucky enough to be out in the open.

Almond Blossom tried to keep her

spirits up by practicing the steps of her spring dance, but her heart wasn't in it. Bleakly, she noticed that her fairy outfit was beginning to look very shabby. The pale pink petals of her tutu looked crumpled rather than frothy, while the ones adorning her chestnut locks were damp and bedraggled because of the rain. As for her dusky pink tunic, it had most definitely seen better days. Tansy— who was a whiz with needle and thread— offered to repair her clothes with some of

Snowdrop's snowy white petals, but Almond Blossom politely refused. It wouldn't feel right wearing someone else's petals. No, she would make herself a brand-new outfit when her own blossoms bloomed. Just as she did every year.

Then the crisis deepened. One murky morning, when the weather was so dark and gloomy that the Flower Fairies had to use pinches of precious fairy dust to light their way, word spread around the garden that an emergency meeting was to take place at the blackthorn bush.

As soon as she heard the news, Almond

Blossom hopped down to the ground, smoothed her ragged clothes, and—peeping in a puddle on the way to make sure that she didn't look too scruffy—scurried toward the blackthorn bush. By the time she arrived, a large crowd of Flower Fairies had gathered. They muttered to each other in low voices.

"What's going on?" Almond Blossom asked Windflower, an elegant fairy with

long, dark hair and mahogany-patterned wings.

Windflower shrugged. "I heard there was going to be some big announcement," she said. "But I haven't a clue what it's about."

"Shhhh!" whispered Blackthorn. She sat on a low branch, almost hidden by the tiny white flowers that smothered her plant—one of the very few to bear flowers in this chilly weather. "Someone's coming!"

"Greetings!" A powerful voice rang out,

silencing the waiting crowd immediately.
Heads swiveled round to see who had
spoken, and then there was a collective gasp.
A dazzling Flower Fairy stood before them.
He was clothed in shimmering gold and
wore a crown of yellow
flower stamens on his
golden hair. It was
Kingcup—the king
of the Flower Fairies!
"Please be seated,"
the royal visitor
continued.

Obediently,
everyone sat.

Almond Blossom's
throat was as dry as
sandpaper, and she
swallowed with
difficulty. It didn't

take a fairy diploma to know that bad news
was coming.

"Flower Fairies . . . we have a problem,"
said Kingcup, his kind eyes clouded with
concern. "I'm sure you've noticed that winter
has gone on for a very long time. For some
weeks, I was convinced that it was just an
odd weather pattern and that any day we'd
see dear Almond Blossom dancing merrily
through the garden, followed swiftly by

glorious spring weather." He paused to smile briefly at her. "But now I know different. Prepare yourselves, Flower Fairies, for the truth is shocking."

Everyone held their breath.

"Spring isn't late," said Kingcup. *"Spring has been stolen!"*

Chapter Two
A Grand Plan

There was a stunned silence as the fairies absorbed the awful news. This wasn't the sort of thing that happened in the Flower Fairies Garden.

"I'm afraid there's more," said Kingcup apologetically. "Unfortunately, this year's Spring Party will have to be postponed ... until spring is restored to its rightful place. I'm most terribly sorry."

There was a strangled sob in the middle of the crowd as one Flower Fairy was overwhelmed by the bad tidings.

Shakily, Almond Blossom raised an arm into the air. "If you please, sir ..." she began.

Kingcup looked in her direction and nodded.

"It's just that ... er ... what I-I-I'd like to know ... that is, what I'm sure *everyone* w-would like to know is ..." Almond Blossom paused, wishing that she felt braver. "How do you know? Why was spring stolen? Who did it? When? And where—"

"Whoa there," said Kingcup, his handsome face creasing into a brief smile. "Let me try to answer those questions before you think of any more." He reached into a pocket and pulled out a scroll of parchment tied with a long ribbon of grass. Slowly, thoughtfully, he held the parchment aloft. "This," he said, "is a ransom note. It explains everything—I think it's best if I read it aloud."

There were nods of approval from the crowd.

Dear Flower Fairies

My, what a long, cold winter! And do you know why? It's because we've stolen spring and hidden it from you. Ha ha! You'll never find it. But we're prepared to do a deal. In exchange for spring, we want six sacks filled to the brim with fairy dust.

On Saturday evening at sunset, you must leave these sacks beneath the almond tree. By Sunday morning, spring will return. No fairy dust means no spring.

Do not try to find us, or we will steal summer too.

Signed,

As if we'd tell you!

Kingcup rolled up the parchment and tucked it back into his pocket. "So, dear Flower Fairies," he said, "we have these dastardly thieves to thank for our worst ever winter. And now we need to work out what to do."

"Why that's simple!" piped up Rose, a friendly little fairy who loved to make others happy. "If everyone works extra hard, we should just about have enough fairy dust by Saturday. I have some large leaves that we could make into sturdy sacks. And perhaps the blackbirds would help by carrying the sacks from flower to flower until they are full."

"No way!" Sycamore cried indignantly. He leaped to his feet and looked stern. "We can't give in to their demands! We must send out a search party immediately and hunt high and low until we've tracked down the thieves."

"But then they'll steal summer!" wailed Daisy.

"I-I-I'm not sure we can make s-six sacks of f-fairy dust by S-S-Saturday." White Clover's round, rosy cheeks were awash with tears.

"We want to go to the Spring Party!" sobbed the Sweet Pea babies.

It was pandemonium. Everywhere Almond Blossom looked, there were Flower Fairies shouting or crying into their petal handkerchiefs. She looked around for Kingcup and saw that he was refereeing a squabble between Yew fairy and Pine Tree fairy. She scratched her head thoughtfully. If they were going to rescue spring *and* save the party, somebody needed to do something right now.

"Please be quiet!" bellowed Almond Blossom at the top of her voice. And

everyone was so astonished by the
mild-mannered fairy's command that they
stopped shouting and arguing and crying
immediately. "Thank you," she continued
meekly. "I have a plan, if anyone would
like to hear it?"

At once, a sea of heads nodded.

"Gather round," whispered Almond Blossom. "We don't want to be overheard."

By noon, it was settled. Most of the Flower Fairies would set to work making heaps of sparkling fairy dust. They decided it would be best if they obeyed the ransom letter's demands—or at least pretended to. Any enemy spies that might be lurking would be fooled into thinking that the fairies had given in, while meanwhile . . .

Almond Blossom would search for spring!

"Aren't you even a tiny bit nervous?"

asked Windflower,
watching as Almond
Blossom packed a small bag
with fairy cheese, hazelnuts, and a
nutcase filled with Elderberry's sweet
juice.

Almond Blossom checked all around
before nodding. "Oh *yes*!" she said. "But I'm
excited too." It was true. She'd never done
anything like this before—never been on a
secret mission, never been trusted with such
an important task. She could hardly wait!

"What will you do?" asked Windflower.
"Where will you go?" Of all the Flower
Fairies, she was perhaps the most eager
for Almond Blossom to succeed, for her
starlike, white flowers would appear when
the first breeze of spring blew.

"First, I'm going to search the Flower
Fairies Garden thoroughly," replied Almond

Blossom, "just to make sure the thieves left no clues. Then I'll travel farther afield—and I won't stop until I've found spring." She smiled at Windflower as she shouldered her bag. "Don't worry—the blackbirds are going to fly above me. If I need help, I'll whistle for them."

"Take this," Windflower said hastily, thrusting a small, silky-soft bag

into her friend's hand. "It's fairy dust. It's not much, I'm afraid, but it's all I have. Go on, run—and take care!" She leaped from the bare branch and somersaulted through the air, landing neatly on the ground below. "Farewell!" she cried, before hurrying away.

Almond Blossom smiled as she looked at Windflower's gift. Everybody was being so kind—she just hoped that she could repay them by returning with spring.

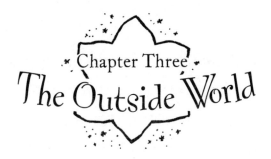

Chapter Three
The Outside World

By the time Almond Blossom had finished
exploring the Flower Fairies Garden, not
a leaf or a stone or a fallen petal was left
unturned. But she didn't find a single clue.
Whoever had stolen spring had done a *very*
good job of covering their tracks.

It's time to go over the wall, thought Almond
Blossom, trudging toward the far side of
the garden. Here, the wall backed onto open
marshes, where only the occasional winding
lane interrupted the wild countryside.
Flower Fairies lived here too—among the
reeds and wild grasses and nestling under
flowers of the hedgerow and wayside. Many
of these fairies visited the garden from time

to time. Almond Blossom hoped to bump into them on her travels—it would be lovely to see a friendly face or two.

She gazed up at the ancient wall, relieved to see that there were plenty of hollows to slip her fingers and toes inside. Briskly, she climbed up the rough stones, stopping only when she reached the top.

"Phew!" said Almond Blossom, perching on the wall to admire the view. Far below her dangling feet was a wide, muddy track, its surface furrowed and uneven. Through the light mist that hung before her, she

could make out a dark green hedgerow opposite. It was interwoven with bindweed—white, cushiony blooms that were bold enough and pushy enough to grow absolutely anywhere. She was wondering if White Bindweed fairy was at home when a wisp of white mist engulfed her. Brrrr! She shivered at its cold touch. It seemed as if the rest of Flower Fairyland was in winter's steely grip too. Almond Blossom couldn't help feeling a little disappointed—she'd hoped that there might be a smidgen of warmth on the other side of the wall.

Ding ding! Ding-a-ling! Ding!
Abruptly, the silence of the quiet

countryside was shattered by a frantic jangling of bells.

"Hurry up, Mark!" The anxious voice echoed along the track, accompanied by more *ding-a-ling*-ing. "We'll be late!"

"I'm coming!" replied another voice.

Humans! She'd never seen or heard one before, but others had told her how big and noisy they were. And according to Flower Fairy law, she *must* stay out of sight. If humans knew that fairies really did exist, the fairies' fragile world might be crushed underfoot by stampeding feet or harmed by curious fingers.

With nowhere to hide and no time to flee, Almond Blossom had no choice but to fold her wings shut and curl herself into the tightest possible ball. And then she waited.

The ground began to tremble horribly and there was an ear-splitting screech. "I *really* need new brakes," muttered a voice. The Flower Fairy couldn't resist peeking and saw a girl with dark, silky hair and big blue eyes. She was crouching over a bright blue contraption that Almond Blossom knew must be a bicycle. The girl's face broke into a wide grin as a younger boy skidded to a halt

beside her. They looked so much alike that they had to be sister and brother. "Where's Toby?" she asked.

"Not far away," replied the boy. "He was barking at some mushrooms a little way back. Oh, here he comes!"

A caramel-colored dog with floppy ears bounded out of the mist, sitting—*splat!*—in a puddle beside the children. He panted, his tongue lolling to one side.

I don't know what all the fuss is about, Almond Blossom thought to herself. *Humans seem perfectly harmless. Pleasant, even. And I rather like their d—*

Woof! Woof-woof!
Toby the dog had begun to make the most awful racket that she'd ever

heard. *Ow-ow-ow-WOOOOO!* he howled.

Almond Blossom's heart sank as, too late, she remembered how finely tuned animals' senses were. Now the dog was staring right at Almond Blossom. He'd seen her!

"What is it, Toby?" asked the boy. "You silly dog! There aren't any mushrooms up there . . . or *are* there?" He stood on tiptoe and squinted at the top of the wall.

Any second now, they would start clambering toward her, and then they would find her, and before nightfall she would be on display in a museum—Almond Blossom just knew it! Unless . . . Quickly, she delved her hand deep into the silken bag that

Windflower had given her. She scooped a handful of the precious fairy dust into her palm and blew with all her might.

Whoosh!

A cloud of tiny pollen fragments billowed outward.

"Fairy dust, fairy dust, hide me from sight!" Almond Blossom whispered. At once, the air all around her began to glimmer and shimmer magically.

"What are you looking at, Mark?" asked the girl curiously.

"Er . . . nothing," replied her brother.

"I could have sworn that I saw something . . ."
He paused and frowned, scratching his head.
"Something really strange. But now it's gone.
I must have been mistaken."

Toby the dog had stopped barking now

and was happily snuffling at the children's
feet.

Almond Blossom smiled to herself.
"Thank you, Windflower," she whispered
in the tiniest of voices. The fairy dust had
worked its magic brilliantly—she was *totally*
shielded from view.

"Come on, then," said the girl. "Let's
escape this murky weather—I want to see the
sun again." She leaped back onto her bicycle.
"Race you?"

As the children and their dog vanished around the corner, Almond Blossom rubbed her chin thoughtfully. Something was bothering her, but she couldn't for the life of her work out what it was.

Chapter Four
A Big Adventure

Almond Blossom peered into the darkening gloom. This was not good. Night was falling and she hadn't even reached the marsh yet. And with only two days to go before Saturday's deadline, she didn't have a moment to lose. She grasped a piece of ivy that clung to the stone wall and expertly slid down its length, landing with a tiny *splish* on the sodden ground below.

Shouldering her bag once more, she skipped and fluttered across the track to the safety of the hedgerow.

"Yoohoo!" shouted White Bindweed, who was busy weaving flowers in and out of the hedge. "Are you staying for tea?"

"That's very kind of you," replied Almond Blossom, "but I can't stop. I'm searching for spring."

"Oh, I see . . ." said White Bindweed, screwing up her face as if she didn't really see at all. She shrugged and grinned. "Okay, then. Catch you later!"

Almond Blossom fought her way through the hedge, which for someone as small as a Flower Fairy was more like a huge and very spooky forbidden forest. Sturdy branches blocked her path, while twigs sprang at her and tore her already tattered clothes. And it was *so* dark. Bravely she pushed on, reminding herself that the happiness of the Flower Fairies *and* the magnificent Spring Party were at stake. She *had* to succeed.

At last, she reached the other side of the hedge. The overcast sky was charcoal gray now—soon it would be black—but there was just enough light for Almond Blossom to see a little way. She plunked herself down on a handy rock and admired the view. So this was the fabled marsh. A carpet of moss stretched away from her, dotted with clumps of tall grass. Large, lumpy shapes loomed in the distance. For a moment, she feared they might be giants or ogres or some other scary creatures, but then she realized that

they were probably just trees. She giggled to herself, as excitement fizzed through her once more.

This was a grand adventure, all right.

"Time to go!" she announced to the empty wilderness. She leaped to her feet and marched away from the hedge, trying hard not to lose her balance on the springy moss.

Almond Blossom soon learned that while the Flower Fairies Garden was quite flat, the marsh was a totally different story. Hollows nestled between grassy hillocks, some of which were mountainous. She struggled to the top of the highest of these mounds, deciding that it would be a perfect spot to camp for the night. But when she reached the top, all thoughts of sleep instantly vanished from her mind.

"What *is* it?" breathed the little Flower Fairy. A bright stripe of sparkling color split the darkness, stretching from left to right across the distant horizon. Almond Blossom had never seen anything so wonderful. It glittered like the brightest jewel and burned as bright as the biggest candle. It was vivid pink and luscious orange and deepest mauve.

It was beautiful.

But she still didn't know what it *was*. Dazzled and bewildered, Almond Blossom sank onto the comfortable moss and stared. Little by little, the mysterious glow faded from view, the colors darkening, the light dimming ... until it was gone. Then, tired beyond belief, she slept.

"Wakey, wakey, rise and shine!" sang a friendly voice.

"Hmmm?" groaned Almond Blossom. She looked up groggily to see two of the scruffiest Flower Fairies she'd ever laid eyes on staring down at her. "Who are you?" she asked.

"I'm Rush-Grass," announced the dark-haired fairy. He reached down to shake Almond Blossom's hand, pumping it up and down enthusiastically. "Pleased to meet you."

"And I'm Cotton-Grass," said the other fairy, with a cheeky grin. His hair was ash

blond and stood up from his head as if he'd had a very big fright. "We're brothers."

Almond Blossom smiled back, noticing absentmindedly that the two Flower Fairies

had *very* pointy ears. And although their wings were quite plain, their clothes blended in perfectly with the colors of the marsh grasses—chestnut brown, moss green, and deep maroon. In fact, they seemed so much at home on the marsh that she knew without asking that they must be locals.

"You're not from around here, are you?"

said Rush-Grass, reminding her that she hadn't introduced herself yet.

"Oh, I'm sorry," she said. "How very rude of me. I'm Almond Blossom—I come from the Flower Fairies Garden." She sprang to her feet and curtsied politely.

"There's no need for that," said Cotton-Grass, with a stifled giggle. "You're on the marsh now—we're much more laid back here than the fairies in your garden." He gave his brother a sideways glance. "Are *you* going to ask her?"

Rush-Grass nodded. "What are you *doing* here?" he asked curiously. "Are you lost? Because if you're lost, we'd be delighted to lead you to safety. That's our job, you see."

Almond Blossom shook her head.

"And if you're *not* lost," added Cotton-Grass, "then we're pretty good guides too. We can show you all the sights—the twisty marsh path, the fairy rings, the elves' secret hideaway, Mallow's famous fairy cheese—"

"What?" Almond Blossom spluttered. Of course! How could she have been so forgetful?

"It's delicious," said Cotton-Grass, rubbing his tummy and making *mmmmm* noises. "Mallow's seeds make the most

 excellent cheese—the best in Flower Fairyland—"

"No, not the *cheese*," interrupted Almond Blossom again. "The elves!

Can you help me to find them?"

"But of course," replied Rush-Grass. He gave an exasperated sigh and rolled his eyes. "What have they done now?" he asked.

"Well, they may have done *nothing*," began Almond Blossom uncertainly. She was a very fair fairy and liked to give everyone a chance, but the elves were well known throughout the Flower Fairies Garden for their tricks and monkey business. Stealing spring would be just the sort of mischief they loved. "I have a feeling that they might be able to point me in the right direction," she added. Noticing that the brothers were looking quite confused, Almond Blossom told them how the Flower Fairies had received a ransom note and there were no clues in their garden, so she'd ventured over the wall and onto the marsh to search for any sign of spring or the wicked thieves who'd stolen it. "Surely you must have noticed how long winter has lasted?" she said.

"Oh, yes," said Cotton-Grass. "The weather's dreadful here, isn't it?" He looked up at the thick gray clouds above them. "It's much nicer on the other side of the marsh. We should take you there." He pointed. "Look!"

Almond Blossom looked. She blinked. Then she looked again. There, in the distance, was a sunny strip of yellow, just visible at the edge of the low, gray cloud. Was it . . . ? Could it really be . . . ? It was!

"Hurray!" she cheered, fluttering into the air with joy. "It's springtime! We've found *spring*!"

Chapter Five
Caught!

At once, everything slotted into place...
Spring hadn't been stolen—it was simply
hidden behind a thick blanket of gray cloud.
This explained why the children had hurried
to escape the murky weather and find the
sun. It also explained why it seemed as if
winter had lasted so long this year.

"The beautiful stripe of color was the
sunset," breathed Almond Blossom. It
was such an age since she'd
seen the evening sun, she'd
forgotten how magnificent it
could be. She was so pleased
that she couldn't resist a
happy skip and a hop,
much to the delight of

her new fairy friends.

Then she sat down and thought. And thought. But no matter how she puzzled and pondered, mused and mulled it over, she kept coming back to the same conclusion. Whoever had sent the ransom note to the Flower Fairies must *also* have hung the great dark cloud above their garden.

"Will you help me to find the thieves?" she asked the marsh fairies. "I want to ask the elves what they know, but I don't know where to find them."

Rush-Grass and Cotton-Grass nodded solemnly.

"We'll take you there as soon as you've had breakfast," said Rush-Grass sensibly. "It's really not a good idea to do this sort of thing on an empty stomach."

So as soon as Almond Blossom had nibbled a hazelnut and sipped the cool spring

water that Cotton-Grass had brought her, they set off across the marsh. They trekked past tall waving grasses and around squidgy bogs, the two brothers making sure that she

didn't stray away from the path and into
danger.

It didn't take long to reach the edge of
the cloud, where the marsh was bathed in
glorious sunshine. Almond Blossom paused
for a moment, closing her eyes and raising
her face up to the gentle warmth of the sun.

"There," Cotton-Grass whispered.

Almond Blossom blinked a little as her
eyes got used to the brightness. "Where?"
she whispered back, scanning the area all
around them.

Cotton-Grass pointed to an innocent-looking cluster of toadstools a short distance away.

They were quite the prettiest things Almond Blossom had seen all morning, with their chocolatey-brown stems and their cherry-red caps, dotted all over with large white spots. The colors dazzled in the spring sunshine.

"Quite poisonous, of course," muttered Rush-Grass. "And the perfect place for those naughty elves to hide their secret headquarters."

"We don't *know* that they've done anything wrong," said Almond Blossom.

"Hmmm." Cotton-Grass didn't sound so sure. "Then let's go and find out," he said, marching toward the toadstools. But before they even reached the elves' secret hideaway, gleeful voices rang out loud and clear.

"We've *fooled* them!"

"Tomorrow we'll have *six sacks* of fairy dust!"

"We are *so* clever! Ha ha *haaa*!"

Almond Blossom crept closer and peered between the toadstools. And there, in a small clearing, were three green-clad creatures with pointy ears and pointy wings. They were laughing fit to burst. "You're not that clever," she said sweetly.

The elves spun around. "Oh," said the tallest of the three.

"Oh, indeed," said Almond Blossom, squeezing through a narrow gap into the hideaway. She put her hands on her hips and frowned at the guilty-looking trio. "Why did you do it?" she asked.

"We only wanted some fairy dust,"

mumbled the shortest elf, staring down at
his feet. "It's not fair, you know," he said.

"You Flower Fairies have all the fun, with
your singing and dancing in your *wonderful*
garden."

He looked up and glared at Almond
Blossom, who was suddenly feeling a little
sorry for the miserable creatures.

"We thought it would be funny if we were enjoying the lovely spring weather, while you were stuck under a wintry cloud," he continued. "And it *was* funny. We haven't been able to *stop* laughing." He looked at his two sidekicks. "Have we, lads?"

"Er, yes . . ." said the tall elf quickly. "I mean, no, boss."

"Ho ho ho," the third elf laughed unconvincingly. "Hee hee."

"But why did you write the ransom note?" asked Almond Blossom, curious now. "Why didn't you just hide the sun and be done with it? Why did you want the fairy dust too? Elves have their own magic

60

dust, don't they?"

"It's not as sparkly as yours," grumbled the chief elf. "And it's not quite as magical either. Besides, we've only got about a thimbleful left—it took heaps of elf dust to cast the Winter Cloud Spell." He paused and looked suddenly cunning. "Why don't you tell us how to make fairy dust? Because if we knew how to make it, we wouldn't need yours, would we?"

"Nice try!" Almond Blossom laughed. "But I'm afraid that only Flower Fairies can make fairy dust—and how we make it is a closely guarded secret."

"Hmmmph," said the elf.

Almond Blossom thought deeply. Here was a problem indeed. How was she to convince the elves to lift the cloud that covered the Flower Fairies Garden *without* collecting the six sacks of fairy dust they'd demanded? Unless . . .

Almond Blossom pulled out the silky bag that Windflower had given her. "Listen very carefully," she said mysteriously. "I have an idea."

Chapter Six
Back to the Garden

Almond Blossom ran her fingertips over her velvet-soft tunic and gently touched the tiny petals sewn around the neck. Then she whirled around, grinning with delight as the pink petals of her skirt spun outward. Her new outfit was perfect.

She was ready.

Carefully breaking off a twig from her tree—she made sure to choose one that was heavily laden with brand-new blossoms—

Almond Blossom
clutched it tightly
before leaping into the air.
Gracefully, she fluttered
downward, landing lightly far
below, where green shoots were
beginning to poke through the soil.
Almond Blossom raised herself on
tiptoes, took a deep breath, and began to
sing the words that the Flower Fairies had
waited so long to hear:

"*Joy! The Winter's nearly gone!*
Soon will Spring come dancing on;
And before her, here dance I,
Pink like sunrise in the sky.
Other lovely things will follow;
Soon will cuckoo come, and swallow;
Birds will sing and buds will burst,
But the Almond is the first!"

Happily, she danced through the garden, twirling and high-stepping as she went, hopping and leaping, spinning and swaying.

"Almond Blossom!" cried Sycamore as she jigged past. "Am I glad to see you! Does this mean that spring is officially on the way?"

In reply, she pointed to the east, where the early morning sun was rising above the horizon, turning the wispy clouds above them the same shade of pink as her pretty blossoms.

"Hurray!" cheered Sycamore, bouncing up and down on a branch. Then he stopped. "But what happened to the nasty winter weather? Did we

pay the
ransom?"
"Oh,
I don't
think so,"
Almond
Blossom said
gaily. "There must
be something in the
air, I suppose." She waved her flowery twig.
"Must dash! Don't forget about the Spring
Party!" She chuckled gleefully as she danced
away, leaving a stunned Sycamore behind
her.

Everything had turned out so well.
Understandably, the elves had been dubious
about her idea at first. They were utterly
dazzled by the expectation of the six
wonderful sacks of magical fairy dust that
awaited them, and they were unwilling to

give them up.
But Almond
Blossom had made
them feel so guilty
with stories of the
heartbroken Flower
Fairies with tears
dripping down their
cheeks as they pined
for spring that they
gave in at last and agreed
to lift the Winter Cloud Spell. Because
their stocks of elf dust were so low, Almond
Blossom had handed over the little silken
bag—there were still a couple of handfuls of
Windflower's precious fairy dust left —and
made the elves promise to use it wisely,
before she hitched a lift home with a friendly
blackbird.

Now, as she admired the glorious morning

sky, Almond Blossom saw that the elves had kept their word.

"*Joy! The winter's nearly gone!*" she sang again, continuing her merry dance.

The Flower Fairies were so eager for the new season to arrive that the Spring Party was held only a few days later. The garden was decked with as many flowers as Almond Blossom could spare and bunches of sunny yellow daffodils. Wildflower's tiny white flowers were scattered over the ground like fallen stars, while swathes of newly opened bluebells stretched as far as the eye could see. So much extra fairy dust had been made that week, it was sprinkled here and there. The glade gleamed and twinkled everywhere the Flower Fairies looked.

It was a wonderful party. Lots of familiar faces joined in the fun, but there were some

unfamiliar faces too. Rush-Grass and
Cotton-Grass had made the long journey

across the marsh—they turned out to be
excellent dancers—and three more visitors
weren't far behind.

The elves smiled sheepishly at Almond
Blossom as they sipped Elderberry's famous
juice from buttercups. "Thank you for
inviting us," mumbled the chief elf, fiddling
with his cuff.

"We love to dance," said the second elf, who was unable to stop his feet from tapping.

"We just never get the chance," said the third elf. "Thank you."

"It's the least I could do," Almond Blossom replied. "After all, you did return spring to us!"

And with that she winked at the elves and fluttered across to join her fairy friends at her favorite party of the year.

Visit our Flower Fairies website at:

www.flowerfairies.com

There are lots of fun Flower Fairy games and activities for you to play, plus you can find out more about all your favorite fairy friends!

Log onto the
Flower Fairies
Friendship Ring

Visit the Flower Fairies website to sign up for the new Flower Fairies Friendship Ring!

★ No membership fee
★ News and updates
★ Every new friend receives a special gift!
<small>(while supplies last)</small>

More tales from these Flower Fairies coming soon!

Candytuft

Strawberry

Jasmine

Sweet Pea

This book
belongs to

....

To Rosalie

FREDERICK WARNE

Published by the Penguin Group
Penguin Books Ltd, 80 Strand, London WC2R 0RL, England
Penguin Young Readers Group, 345 Hudson Street,
New York, New York 10014, U.S.A.
Penguin Books Australia Ltd, 250 Camberwell Road, Camberwell,
Victoria 3124, Australia
Canada, India, New Zealand, South Africa

5

Copyright © Frederick Warne & Co., 2006

New reproductions of Cicely Mary Barker's illustrations
copyright © The Estate of Cicely Mary Barker, 1990
Original text and illustrations copyright
© The Estate of Cicely Mary Barker,
1923, 1925, 1926, 1934, 1940, 1944, 1948

All rights reserved

Printed in Great Britain

Rose's Special Secret

by Kay Woodward

Welcome to the Flower Fairy Garden!

Where are the fairies?
Where can we find them?
We've seen the fairy-rings
They leave behind them!

Is it a secret
No one is telling?
Why, in your garden
Surely they're dwelling!

No need for journeying,
Seeking afar:
Where there are flowers,
There fairies are!

Contents

Chapter One
A Narrow Escape

"I'll miss you," Rose whispered softly. The Flower Fairy looked at the tangle of thorns and withered leaves for the very last time. For as long as she could remember, this tatty, overgrown, *wonderful* rosebush had been her home. She'd trimmed and tended its crooked stems, encouraging the ancient plant to send out delicate pink buds every spring and summer. She'd done everything in her power

to take care of it. And in return, the prickly plant had given her soft pink petals to wear and a beautiful place to live. But disaster was approaching—and not even fairy dust could save the rosebush now.

A loud *swoosh* interrupted Rose's

melancholy thoughts, and she glanced up as a sparrow hurtled past, chirping noisily. When she heard what the anxious bird had to say, Rose hastily flung her leafy bag over one shoulder. *They* were on their way. It was time for *her* to go.

"Good-bye," said Rose, a lone tear

trickling down her cheek. "I'll never forget you."

As if saying farewell, the rosebush waved in the breeze.

Feeling that her heart might break, the Flower Fairy gave a brief watery smile, took a deep breath, and then fluttered to the ground. She landed nimbly on dainty feet and hurried in the direction of the morning sun, which was already casting a golden glow over the leafy wilderness that lay before her. As she dodged around weeds and leaped over rocks, Rose's mind whirred.

It had been less than a week since the dreadful rumors had invaded the overgrown garden. The bees had started it, buzzing odd-sounding new words: *Decking. Concrete. Patio.* No one knew what they meant, but they sounded mean, dangerous, and very scary.

Then the human intruders came. They stomped through the garden, crushing delicate flowers and forging wide, muddy pathways with their enormous boots, even uprooting entire plants that had the misfortune to block their way.

Rose and her Flower Fairy friends could no longer hop and flutter freely from flower to flower—they now seemed to spend most of their time scurrying between one leafy plant and the next. They knew, as every Flower Fairy knows, that the only way to make sure that Flower Fairyland remained truly safe was by keeping it very, very secret. The only problem was, their precious homes were disappearing fast—and they were running out of places to hide.

"What are we going to *do*?" Rose cried helplessly to Dandelion. He was one of the toughest, most resourceful Flower Fairies she knew—as well as one of the most brightly dressed. If anyone knew how to deal with these troublesome humans, he would.

"*Do*? Oh, there's nothing we can *do*," Dandelion said matter-of-factly. He swung from one tall rose stem to another, his beautiful yellow-and-black wings almost dazzling Rose with their brilliance. "I've seen it all before. They come. They weed and rake and sow. They roll out carpets of green grass. And then they go. Before long, you have a lovely wilderness once more.'

"But where shall we *go*?" Rose said, her voice trembling. She was trying desperately not to cry, even though everything sounded pretty hopeless.

"It's all right for me," said Dandelion, smoothing down his jaunty yellow-and-green outfit. "It doesn't matter how many times they pull up my flower—it will always grow again. And I'm a bit of a wanderer at heart! But rosebushes . . ." He scratched his head, noticing for perhaps the first time that Rose didn't share his happy-go-lucky mood. "Well . . . if I were you, I'd take a holiday," he suggested kindly. "Go and see a bit of Flower Fairyland. Meet some new Flower Fairies. You might find another rosebush—one even better than this one."

"I'll *never* find a better home than this!" exclaimed Rose. But deep down, she knew that Dandelion was right. Her beloved rosebush wasn't safe any more—and no matter how much she disliked the idea of moving, she *had* to go.

Now, as she rushed toward safety, the tiny Flower Fairy thought she heard the distant sound of metal crunching into dry, cracked earth. Her steps quickened. In no time, she reached the crumbly bricks—covered with masses of pink and peach and lilac blooms— that marked the edge of the world she knew.

Rose looked up and up . . . and up. She'd

been this way once before, but somehow, she
didn't remember the wall being quite this
high. It towered above her, the top so far
away that it was almost out of sight.

Rose flopped down onto a nearby
mushroom, resting the bag on her knee.
Inside, she'd carefully stowed all her
possessions: the petal dress that she kept for
best, a sunny yellow flower that Dandelion
had given her as a going-away present
(he said that it would make an excellent
umbrella), a single pink rosebud to remind

her of her old home, and a tiny gossamer bag of fairy dust. This last item had to be saved for emergencies. But as she peered up at the lofty wall, Rose realized that she would need all her fairy dust to help her fly over this—the very first obstacle that she'd encountered. Once her fairy dust was gone, what would she do *then* for fairy magic? She could make no more fairy dust until she found another rosebush.

"I say," said a soft voice, "you're looking terribly sad. Is there anything I can do to help?"

Rose brushed blonde curls from her eyes and examined the wall more closely. A Flower Fairy was watching her curiously from among gently ruffled pink petals. It was Sweet Pea! She wore a delicate

pink skirt made from layers of the same petals as her flower, and a leaf-green bodice. Her hair was long, dark, and wavy.

"Because if you're wondering about climbing this wall, you needn't worry," Sweet Pea went on. "It's a snap. No need for even the tiniest pinch of fairy dust."

And Rose saw that it was true. The entire wall was covered with curly, green tendrils—ideal handholds and footholds for fairy feet. She grinned widely at the helpful Flower Fairy and picked up her bag once more.

"Come on," said Sweet Pea brightly. "I'll show you the way."

Chapter Two
Over the Wall

"Oooh . . ." breathed Rose. She'd never seen anything like it—ever. From her bird's-eye perch on top of the old wall, she gazed at a whole new world that stretched far into the distance. It looked utterly magical.

"Pretty good, eh?" said Sweet Pea. She sat peacefully beside Rose as she, too, admired the view.

Far below their fairy feet were flowers of

every color and description. There were tall snapdragons, their plump yellow and red blossoms waving in the breeze. Billowing bushes of dusky lavender rustled to and fro, and ground ivy, speckled with tiny lilac flowers, crept along the moss-covered earth. Startlingly pink zinnia flowers stood proudly, while elegant yellow irises clustered along the banks of a sparkling stream.

"Where are we?" whispered Rose, noticing

that Sweet Pea's pink, peach, and lilac flowers spread down this side of the wall, too.

"Why, this is the Flower Fairies' Garden," Sweet Pea announced proudly. "It's beautiful isn't it?"

Rose nodded wordlessly.

"You'll love it here," said Sweet Pea, suddenly distracted by a floaty dandelion seed that wafted past her nose. She peered down at the dandelion clock far below. "Goodness, is that the time?" She leaped to her feet and smoothed down her pink petticoats. "I'd better be going. You take care, won't you?" she added, flinging a leg back over the wall.

"Watch out for el—" she called as she

disappeared.

'What?' Rose called after her. 'Watch out for *what*?'

But Sweet Pea had vanished.

What could she have meant? thought Rose, worry crinkling her pretty forehead for a moment. Then she shrugged—it was probably nothing.

Another dandelion seed whirled past, giving Rose a splendid idea. She flipped open her bag and tugged out Dandelion's gift, admiring the tightly packed yellow petals. It would keep her dry in the rain, but it would catch the breeze too.

"One, two, three, fly!" cried Rose. Holding her dandelion aloft and clutching her bag, she leaped from the wall and soared through the air. Slowly, gracefully, the Flower Fairy

swooped toward the garden, fluttering
her pearly pink wings occasionally to
change direction. As she approached
the ground, her feet skimmed the
topmost blossoms, releasing
delicious, flowery scents.
Lower, lower, lower she
went, until—*thud!*—she
landed on a cushion
of springy moss.
Rose sighed
with relief and
looked around.
All she could see
were flowers—no
Flower Fairies.
Where were
they?
"Well,
hello!" sang a

friendly voice. "Nice of you to drop in!" A
mischievous face popped up from behind
a bristly cornflower and skipped over. His
entire outfit—jerkin, shorts, silken slippers,
and even a crown —was pure, dazzling blue,
made from the starry petals of his flower.
"Welcome to the garden!" he added, bowing
politely and waving a regal hand. "I'm
Cornflower."

Rose clambered to her feet and bobbed a quick curtsey. "Pleased to meet you," she said, trying to ignore the warm blush that she could feel coloring her cheeks. She wasn't used to meeting strangers. "I'm Rose."

"Marvelous," said Cornflower. He looked quizzically at her, taking in the dishevelled clothes and ruffled blonde curls. "I expect you'll want to get settled in," he said helpfully, bending to pick up her bag and dandelion. "Where's your flower?"

Her heart sank. Cornflower was being so kind, so helpful, so welcoming. She didn't know how to tell him that she didn't really belong here—that she didn't have a flower, not anymore. And she didn't even know if there *were* any rosebushes in the Flower Fairies' Garden for her to make her new home. What was she to *do*?

"I'm so sorry, my dear," said Cornflower. "Here I am, yabbering away. And there you are, worn out after your journey. In fact, I bet you're so tired that you can't remember *where* your flower is." He patted her shoulder sympathetically. "I'll help you find it."

"But—" began Rose.

"No buts!" said Cornflower, flinging

Rose's bag over his shoulder and grasping the dandelion as if it
were a floral spear. "Follow me!"

The eager fairy hopped and skipped merrily around the garden, while Rose hurried along in his wake. She tried once or twice more to explain why she was there, but it was no use. Cornflower simply said that there was no need to thank him, and that she should save her breath for the journey.

Eventually, Rose did as she was told, scurrying to keep up with the sprightly Flower Fairy.

As they zigzagged between the flowers, the silent garden seemed magically to come alive. Beautifully camouflaged Flower Fairies popped out from behind blossoms, stems, and clumps of wild grass. They called out friendly greetings as the small procession passed.

Soon, Rose felt quite at home. "Everyone is *so* nice!" she exclaimed happily.

But there was no sign of a rosebush, not even a solitary rosebud. And meanwhile, the sun was moving unstoppably through the summer sky. By teatime, although they had searched most of the Flower Fairy Garden, they were still no closer to finding a place where Rose could lay her head. There remained just one place they hadn't explored.

"Why don't we try over there?" Rose asked, pointing to the dark, forbidding mass of undergrowth in the far corner of the garden.

"Oh, you won't find your rosebush in there," Cornflower said, shaking his head dismissively. "I think perhaps we'll try the area near the forget-me-nots again."

Rose hardly heard. She was far too busy pushing through the thick grasses that crowded in front of her, blocking her view.

She weaved in and out of the tall, emerald blades until eventually she emerged at the other side. There, facing her, was a terribly overgrown thicket. And poking out of the very middle of the thicket—so tiny that most Flower Fairies would have mistaken it for a sharp twig—was a thorn.

A rose thorn.

Rose grinned from ear to ear. "I've found it!" she called happily.

"A rosebush?" said Cornflower, rustling

through the grass to join her. "Really?" He
peered uncertainly at the undergrowth. "It
doesn't look very lived in," he added, looking
at Rose as if thinking that she'd quite clearly
gone mad.

"I'm sure," said Rose. "That's the place."

* * *

As the setting sun cast a rosy glow over
the garden, Rose surveyed her new home.

Cornflower had gone—reluctantly, and
with a great deal of grumbling—after she'd
persuaded him that she really would be
absolutely, totally fine and that he wasn't to
worry and that she would whistle loudly if
even the tiniest thing was wrong. But now the
light was fading fast and Rose realized that
it was getting too dark to see anything at all,
never mind explore.

She heard the gentle breathing of sleeping
Flower Fairies echoing from nearby flowers
and trees. The reassuring sound made her

feel sleepy, and her eyelids began to droop. "I *am* feeling rather tired," she murmured to herself. And using a fallen leaf as a coverlet, she snuggled down in a small grassy hollow. She soon drifted off to sleep. But her dreams were filled with strange mutterings.

Who is she? . . . I don't know! . . . What's she doing here? . . . Don't ask me! . . . Doesn't she know that we live here? . . . I don't know!

Chapter Three
Inside the Rosebush

Rose was awakened bright and early by the chirpy melody of the local lark.

"Morning!" she called out to the little bird. Then, cupping her hands around an acorn shell that had filled with dew during the night, she turned her attention to the overgrown thicket.

A dark, uninviting mass of gnarly stems reared up before her—dark and wild and spiky. Dried, crispy leaves had been blown into the bush by the wind. They plugged every gap, making it difficult to see far inside. Rose wasn't surprised that no one lived here. After thirstily draining the beechnut shell, she set to work.

First she brushed away the old, crinkled leaves. Next she carefully pruned the outermost twigs by sprinkling a touch of fairy dust onto the stems, then nipping them between her fingertips. She couldn't help pausing to admire her handiwork every few moments—the bush was looking neater and healthier already. Better still, it was starting to look like a rosebush, instead of just a heap of tangled twigs. There was still no sign of any roses though.

Then came the exciting bit. Now that she'd cleared the edge of the plant, it was time to venture inside. With small spry steps, Rose made her way to the very heart of the rosebush, pushing springy twigs and branches out of her path. It was farther than she had thought and, to make sure she didn't get lost, she left tiny sparkles of glittering fairy dust along the way. Little by little,

the light grew dim and the sounds from
the garden faded, while Rose grew more
enthusiastic with every step. She was about to
make a great discovery—she just *knew* it.

And then she did.

Suddenly, she burst through a particularly
thorny patch to find that the sun was blazing
down on the other side. And there, before
her, was the loveliest sight she'd ever laid
eyes on. In a small clearing grew a cluster of
dainty rosebushes. All were in full bloom,
their deep-red and soft pink flowers shining
like jewels against the dark green leaves.
There were tiny white rosebuds, too.

"A secret rose garden," breathed Rose. Was she the very first Flower Fairy ever to see this beautiful place? She *must* be. Otherwise, Cornflower would surely have known about it.

At once, her happiness was replaced by heartache. Rose was such a kindly soul that she couldn't bear the thought of these stunning flowers being hidden away where no one could see them. And then a thought pinged into her mind. *What if she were to clear a path through the outer bushes? Then the other Flower Fairies would be able to visit this marvelous place whenever they wanted—without having to battle their way through the spiky, dark undergrowth first.*

"Better still," she said aloud, "I could work some Flower Fairy magic on

the overgrown
rosebush too. With
a little love and
attention, it could
look as wonderful as my
secret gar—!"

A sudden squawking noise
interrupted her wonderful plan. Rose
whipped her head around to see who had
spoken, but there was not a creature in sight.
When a large, glossy crow flew overhead and
cawed loudly, she breathed a sigh of relief
and chuckled to herself. Silly Rose! She was
getting jumpy
for no reason.

Briskly she spun on her heel, ducked into
the undergrowth, and started back the way
she'd come. And as she went, she made plans.
She was going to turn her new home into a
lovely place for everyone to enjoy. And she

would only reveal the secret garden when all the hard work was done. That way, it would be a *real* surprise!

"Ouch!" Rose felt a sharp prickle, and her daydream vanished. She frowned and rubbed her leg. That wasn't supposed to happen—she was the Rose Flower Fairy! Rose thorns never pricked or poked her, not like they pricked and poked the other Flower Fairies who brushed against them. Whether it was because she took care of roses and it was the plants' way of saying thank you, or whether she just had super-tough skin, Rose didn't

know. The point was . . . she didn't *feel* pointy rose thorn things.

"'Tee hee!"

Rose froze and darted quick glances to the left and right. That was no crow. It didn't sound like a Flower Fairy either. Someone was watching her—and laughing at her, too. She looked around frantically. Who could it be?

"That'll teach you to invade elf territory!" said a mocking voice.

Rose whirled to face a strange creature dressed entirely in green. He stood with his

hands planted firmly on his hips, looking
rather pleased with himself.

"Who are you?" she asked bravely.

The green-clad creature gave a short laugh
and clicked his fingers. Instantly, two more
creatures appeared, one on either side of him.
They all stared insolently at Rose, and in the
brief pause that followed, she couldn't

help noticing how long and pointy their ears
were. She also noticed that one of them was
wielding a very sharp twig. So this was who

had prodded her!

"*We,*" said the leader importantly, 'are the elves. And *we* live here.'

"Pleased to meet you," said Rose. In a flash, she remembered Sweet Pea's words before she disappeared over the wall. She must have said, "Watch out for *elves*!" Rose didn't know much about elves, apart from

their reputation for naughtiness and general mischief, but she was determined not to feel nervous. "I live here, too," she added brightly. "I'm sure there's room enough for all of us."

"Ha!" barked the first elf. "But it's going to be no fun for us if you tidy everything up and

make it all light and airy and *nice*." He said
the last word as if it were a bad thing.
"*We* like it dark and tangled. *We* are the
elves."

"Yes," said Rose wearily. "You said." She
tried again, her sky blue eyes pleading with
them to understand. "The thing is, I'm Rose
and it's my job as a Flower Fairy to take care
of this neglected old plant. I've escaped from
humans and decking and concrete and patios
and *chaos* to come here. My old home is about
to be pruned, or worse."

"Chaos?" It appeared that of all Rose had
said, the bossy elf had heard just one word.
"Where is this place?" he demanded. "*We* like
chaos. *We* are th—"

"Yes, yes," said Rose hurriedly. "It's just over the wall at the edge of the Flower Fairies' Garden."

The elves' dark, beady eyes glittered. As if triggered by some unseen signal, the trio huddled together and spoke quickly in low, excited voices. Then they faced Rose. "We've decided," said the leader importantly. "You can keep your rosebush. *We're* going to make mischief."

Rose barely had time to nod before the three elves shot past her, the speed of their departure spinning her around on the spot. "Be nice to Dandelion, won't you?" she called after them.

"What do you take us for?" The indignant reply came from far away. "We're not the pixies, you know!"

Laughing with relief, Rose followed her glittering trail back through the overgrown rosebush to the outside world. Now that she'd solved the mystery of the muttering voices and said good-bye to the twig-wielding elves, she was free to get on with what she did best—tending to rosebushes.

Chapter Four
A Magical Transformation

It was hard work, but Rose loved it. Politely refusing all offers of help, she spent her days pruning and trimming and neatening up the overgrown corner of the Flower Fairies' Garden. And whenever anyone asked for a guided tour, she simply flashed them a twinkly smile and tapped her nose. "Wait and see," was all she would say. Not even Cornflower's gentle teasing could entice her to reveal more.

Each evening, when she was tired—and very happy—Rose got to know the other Flower Fairies. They were very kind, inviting her to munch on tasty mallow seeds—a special sort of fairy cheese—and brewing her fresh cups of elderberry tea. While she ate and drank, different fairies entertained her with stories from the Flower Fairy Garden. Rose hadn't realized so many charming

creatures lived there, and slowly she got to know each and every one. She was having a *marvelous* time.

The days went by. And, by the time the moon had grown from a thin, silvery sliver into a large shining ball and shrunk back to a sliver, Rose realized—with some surprise—that her work was nearly done. The overgrown corner of the garden had been utterly transformed. Gone were the long, tangled stems and withered leaves. In their place were healthy, young stems and fresh, green foliage.

Meanwhile, excitement in the garden had reached fever pitch. Although the Flower Fairies loved surprises, that didn't stop them from wondering endlessly what the hard-working fairy was up to. One day, Rose overheard two of the youngest Flower Fairies—White Clover and Heather— earnestly discussing the topic.

"I think she's practising circus tricks," said White Clover, a little fairy with round rosy cheeks. "She's learning to juggle with hazelnuts, where no one can see. That way, it's not embarrassing when she drops her nuts."

Heather wasn't convinced. "I think she's making rugs," he said knowledgeably. "She's collecting all of these old twigs so that she can weave them together. When Rose lets us inside the bush, we'll find that she's made a huge, twiggy carpet."

Rose covered her mouth to stifle a giggle, before hurrying away down the neat and tidy new path that she'd tunnelled through the rosebush. Little did the Flower Fairies know that not one but *two* surprises awaited them.

As well as tending the rosebushes, she had been busily collecting old petals to make rosewater. After collecting dew inside a large chestnut shell, Rose had added the petals to make a pink soup. Today, she was going to turn the soup into rosewater!

Carefully she climbed into the chestnut shell, which was wedged securely into a clump of moss to make sure that it didn't tip over. Lifting her left foot, then right, left, right, she squooshed and squished her toes into the water and petal mixture, turning it into a flowery mush.

"Mmmmm..." Rose sighed, as a beautiful smell began to drift upward. This rosewater would be the perfect way to thank the kind Flower Fairies for letting her stay in their garden. *Everything's ready*, she thought happily.

That evening, Rose hopped, skipped, and fluttered from flower to flower, inviting everyone to the far corner of the Flower Fairies' Garden the next day. Everyone was very excited, none more so than Cornflower, who regarded Rose as his special friend.

"Yes, yes," he said loudly to anyone who would listen. 'It's all going to be a wonderful surprise, with lots of marvelousness and fabulous splendifery. You won't believe your eyes. Just wait and see!"

Honeysuckle, who was perched high on a curling tendril, grinned broadly. "You don't have a clue what's going on, do you?" he said, with a chuckle.

"Er . . . I . . . er . . . well, er . . . no," admitted
Cornflower truthfully. "But I bet it's
wonderful, all the same!"

He was right.

The next day dawned bright and clear, with
not a cloud in the sapphire blue sky. Birds
twittered cheerily from the branches of the
silver birch tree. And the sun soon chased
away the delicate wisps of mist that lingered
near the ground.

Nervously smoothing down her best dress,
Rose sat next to the rosebush that had once
been so neglected and unloved. Now, it was

a mass of green foliage. In the last day or two, tiny white-and-pink rosebuds had even begun to appear, like stars twinkling in a night sky.

Cornflower was the first to arrive. "All sorted?" he asked eagerly.

Rose nodded. There was something she needed to say—she just wasn't quite sure how to say it. Or how Cornflower would react. She took the plunge.

"The thing is, Cornflower . . . when we first met, I should have said that I didn't actually belong in the garden and that I didn't have a flower. It was just lucky that we found this rosebush—but, really, it's not mine." She didn't dare look up. "And I quite understand if you want me to leave the Flower Fairies' Garden, but I just want you to know that I love it here and—"

"Whoa there!" said Cornflower, flapping his gauzy blue wings. "Why did you think any of that would matter?" he asked, with a totally bemused expression. "We welcome all Flower Fairies into the garden, *wherever* in Flower Fairyland they come from." He raised a finger to his lips when Rose tried to speak again. "Now, not another word! This is your home now."

She smiled gratefully.

Then, one by one, more Flower Fairies

started to arrive, their faces bright with curiosity. There was Zinnia and Wild Cherry. Candytuft came next, then Lavender and Elder. Soon, everyone was there—the air buzzing with anticipation.

Rose clambered onto a toadstool so that she could see everyone. "I'd like to thank you all," she began quietly.

"Catch!" shouted Honeysuckle, throwing her one of his pinky-orange flowers. "Speak into that," he added. "Then we'll all be able to hear you!"

Rose smiled and put the trumpet-shaped flower to her lips.

"You've made me so welcome," she went on. "So I'd like to welcome you to my secret garden. Except I don't want it to be a secret anymore. I want it to be a place for Flower Fairies to enjoy."

"Hurray!" shouted Cornflower.

"You've still no idea what's going on, have you?" Honeysuckle laughed.

"Nope!" said Cornflower, shrugging his shoulders. "But it's very exciting, all the same!"

"This way," said Rose, leaping down from her toadstool and tugging aside a large leaf that she'd positioned in front of the tunnel

entrance. Then she stepped inside.

The way was leafy green and dappled with the sunlight that filtered through the rosebush. Rose had done so much pruning that the once dark and forbidding bush was light and airy. And the other Flower Fairies had no need to fear thorns—Rose had carefully twisted the stems so that the prickles pointed the other way. Ooohing and aaahing in wonder, they followed Rose deeper and deeper, until ...

"*Wow*!" said Cornflower, as he emerged into daylight.

"*Amazing!*"

"*Unbelievable!*"

Exclamations of delight echoed around Rose's secret garden as the bedazzled Flower Fairies took

in the view. Rose had nipped and shaped
the dainty rosebushes until they were each
a perfect ball. Any wilting flowers had been
removed, leaving only the newest, freshest
blooms. The large, dark red flowers looked
as if their petals were made of velvet, while
the pale pink and white rosebuds looked like
soft marshmallows.

"And what's this?" asked Cornflower,
dunking his finger into the chestnut
shell. "Mmmm . . . That smells
delicious!"

"It's rosewater," said Rose
shyly. "Dab it on your wrists
and behind your ears—you'll
smell wonderful." She
looked at the others. "It's
for everyone to try," she
said.

They didn't need

telling twice. Soon the air was filled with the beautiful aroma of roses and the sound of happy Flower Fairies as they explored the new garden.

But for Rose, the very best part of the day didn't come until much later. She was relaxing happily among the leaves of the rose garden, thinking how much she loved her brand-new home, when she heard a pattering of tiny fairy feet. She peeped round a deep red rosebud to find Clover and Heather looking back at her.

"We've got a surprise for you," said Clover proudly.

"It's a poem," Heather chipped in.

"We wrote it," added Clover.

Then, before Rose had time to say a word, they began to recite the sweetest verse that she'd ever heard.

Best and dearest flower that grows,
Perfect both to see and smell;
Words can never, never tell
Half the beauty of a rose—
Buds that open to disclose
Fold on fold of purest white,
Lovely pink, or red that glows
Deep, sweet-scented. What delight
To be Fairy of the rose.

"I can't thank you enough," Rose breathed.

"Oh, don't mention it," said Clover, suddenly bashful. 'You've given us so much loveliness, we just wanted to give something to *you*.'

Chapter Five

A Surprise Visitor

For weeks afterwards, all anyone could talk
about was the grand opening of the rose
garden. It became an even more popular
topic than the weather forecast—something
that all Flower Fairies love to talk about.
Gradually, the word spread beyond the
garden to the marshland—a wet, grassy place
that was teaming with dragonflies, minnows,
and frogs. It was also the home of the
Queen of the Meadow Fairy.
Together with Kingcup, she
ruled Flower Fairyland
firmly yet fairly. She
listened to the news of
Rose's surprise with
interest.

"I think perhaps that *I* should pay a visit to this garden," the queen mused aloud, her forehead puckered into a small frown. At once, she summoned a swallow and hopped onto its feathery back. "To the rose garden!" she commanded.

When the swallow swooped down into the middle of the inner rose garden, Rose was making herself a new party dress from pale-pink petals. She looked up in astonishment at the pretty Flower Fairy who slid gracefully to the ground. A flaxen cloud of hair framed her delicate features. She was clad in a silken ivory-colored gown, and round her neck was a necklace of large, green pearls.

"I'm the Queen of the Meadow," said the fairy. She stretched out an elegant hand and grasped Rose's trembling fingers.

"P-p-pleased to meet you," stammered Rose, frantically scouring her mind for things that she might have done wrong. Otherwise, why would the queen of the whole of Flower Fairyland have bothered to come *here*?

"I'd like to look around," said the queen, her blue eyes sweeping left and right. "Would you show me your garden?"

"Why, of c-c-course, Your Royal F-Fairyness!" said Rose. At once, she realised what must be wrong. Obviously, the queen was cross with Rose for disturbing this corner of the garden. She must have preferred it when the roses were overgrown! But there was no sign of a royal telling-off—yet. The queen simply nodded, following Rose around the sculpted rosebushes.

And that was the exact moment the three elves chose to return from their travels. Giggling to themselves, they waited until the two Flower Fairies were out of sight before randomly plucking petals from the nearest bushes and scattering them on the ground.

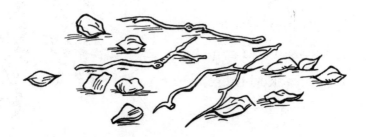

"Tee hee!" chuckled the elf in charge. "So messy!" His fellow elves nudged each other, then shook with silent laughter. When they heard voices approaching, they all hid.

"Oh!" gasped Rose, when she saw the torn petals. "I'm terribly sorry, Your Highness. The flowers are usually so neat. I don't know what happened."

The queen raised an eyebrow, but said nothing.

"I'll show you the secret tunnel," said Rose, desperate to impress the royal visitor, who she was sure must be seriously underwhelmed by now. She took Queen of the Meadow to the tunnel and led her inside.

"Pee-ew!" spluttered Rose. The tunnel smelt *awful*—as if a dozen bad eggs had been cracked there.

The queen wrinkled her nose in disapproval, but remained silent. The final straw came when she went to step back into the secret garden. A long stem suddenly shot out from the side of the tunnel, tripping her up. It was only the timely sprinkling of a little fairy dust that stopped Queen of the Meadow from sprawling on the grass.

"You can come out now," said the queen sternly, standing with her hands on her hips.

Rose popped her head out of the rosebush. "I'm sorry …" she began.

"No, not *you*," said the royal visitor tartly. Her arms were folded and she looked very cross. Suddenly, her voice softened and she pointed at three familiar figures who were now creeping out of the rosebush, their expressions sullen. "*Them.*"

"The elves!" exclaimed Rose.

"Well, what have you to say for yourselves?" said the queen, facing the mischievous trio.

The chief elf sighed dramatically. "*We* are the elves," he said petulantly. "*We* do mischief. That's our *job.*"

"Then I suggest you do it somewhere else," replied Queen of the Meadow. "Rose has worked very hard to make this garden such a wonderful place. So unless you want to help with the pruning and weeding and tidying and . . ." She chuckled gaily as the elves spluttered in horror and sprinted back down the tunnel.

"*We* didn't like it here anyway!" they shouted. "It's too pretty!"

The queen turned to Rose, a wide smile

revealing pearly white teeth. "Well done," she said. "I think you've done a marvelous job. This garden is magnificent. Of course, I knew all along it would be—I just wanted to come and admire it for myself." She clicked her fingers and the swallow soared back down to the garden, landing neatly beside her.

"Oh, thank you!" said Rose.

"Farewell!" called Queen of the Meadow. "Keep up the good work!"

Rose waved until her royal visitor was just

a tiny speck in the distance. Then she settled down on a heap of moss and happily carried on with her sewing. She'd lost her old home, but now she'd found a wonderful new one and lots of fantastic Flower Fairy friends, too. Everything in her garden was truly rosy.

Visit our Flower Fairies website at:

www.flowerfairies.com

There are lots of fun Flower Fairy games and activities for you to play, plus you can find out more about all your favorite fairy friends!

Have you logged onto
the Flower Fairies™ Friends
Friendship Ring?

In the land of Fairyopolis every fairy is your friend
and now the Flower Fairies
want to share their secrets with you!

No Membership Fee

Online Fun

Visit **www.flowerfairies.com**
and sign up for the Flower
Fairies Friendship Ring
and you will receive:

❀ Secret Fairy Coded Messages
❀ News and updates
❀ Invitations to special events
❀ Every new friend receives a
   special gift from the Flower Fairies!
   (while supplies last.)

Frederick Warne & Co.
A division of Penguin Young Readers Group

This book
belongs to

....

To George – my own little pixie

FREDERICK WARNE

Published by the Penguin Group
Penguin Books Ltd, 80 Strand, London WC2R oRL, England
Penguin Young Readers Group, 345 Hudson Street,
New York, New York 10014, U.S.A.
Penguin Books Australia Ltd, 250 Camberwell Road, Camberwell,
Victoria 3124, Australia
Canada, India, New Zealand, South Africa

4

Copyright © Frederick Warne & Co., 2006

New reproductions of Cicely Mary Barker's illustrations
copyright © The Estate of Cicely Mary Barker, 1990
Original text and illustrations copyright
© The Estate of Cicely Mary Barker,
1923, 1925, 1926, 1934, 1940, 1944, 1948

All rights reserved

Printed in Great Britain

Wild Cherry Makes a Wish

by Pippa le Quesne

Welcome to the Flower Fairy Garden!

Where are the fairies?
Where can we find them?
We've seen the fairy-rings
They leave behind them!

Is it a secret
No one is telling?
Why, in your garden
Surely they're dwelling!

No need for journeying,
Seeking afar:
Where there are flowers,
There fairies are!

Contents

Chapter One
Wishes and Daydreams

"May I have this dance?" Beech asked, bowing low.

Wild Cherry Blossom felt like a princess as she took the handsome Tree Fairy's hand and let him lead her toward the dance floor. The waltz that the Flower Fairy orchestra had been playing ended, and Wild Cherry was surprised to hear a very familiar tune

start up. If she wasn't mistaken, it was the soft, warbling song of a blackbird—and not one usually heard at the seasonal ball. In fact, it was exactly the same melody as the one that the blackbird who visited her each morning sang.

Wild Cherry opened her eyes and sighed. She was in her tree, and there, just at the end of the branch that she was curled up on, was her daily visitor announcing a new day. She had been dreaming.

The Tree Fairy yawned and stretched,
opening out her delicate pink wings—
jeweled with drops of dew that glistened
in the early morning sunshine. She always
got up at first light, but to make the most of
spring's precious days, she went to bed early,
too. Wild Cherry loved this time of year
when her tree was covered in velvety leaves
and more clusters of pure white blossoms
than she could count. The air all around her
was heavily scented with the promise of wild
cherries. They wouldn't arrive for a couple
of months yet, but the flowers,
the leaves, and even the twigs
carried their perfume.

This morning, however, she was tired. The evening before, she'd attended the Spring Ball and stayed up late into the night. As always, it had been a magnificent occasion—a huge feast that everyone in Flower Fairyland had attended. The fairy court, hidden in a secret clearing in an overgrown patch of the garden, had been a spectacular sight— bustling with fairies in their most gorgeous outfits and lit by hundreds of firefly lanterns. And best of all had been the dancing.

Wild Cherry Blossom had spent the entire evening as close to the dance floor as possible. She'd chatted to all her friends and piled up an acorn bowl several times with mouthwatering fruit jelly and seed cake, but her eyes never left the light-footed fairies that whirled and twirled to the music. She loved dancing more than anything, yet, unlike in her dream, Wild Cherry never dared dance even a single step at one of the seasonal balls.

"If only I were more like Pansy," the Tree Fairy murmured as she got herself ready for the day.

First of all, she folded up the moss blanket that she slept under and tucked it into a nook in the tree trunk. Then she pulled out a twig comb from the pocket of her white dress and teased out the tangles from her wavy chestnut hair.

Finally, she retied the red sash that she wore across her chest and fastened it in a bow at the back.

Like all the Flower Fairies, Wild Cherry Blossom was very pretty. Her cheeks were always rosy, and she had a heart-shaped face, but she often let her hair fall across it, hiding her features. You see, although Wild Cherry had lots of friends, she was really very shy. She frequently visited the Garden Fairies and was not scared to venture out onto the marsh, but what she enjoyed most of all was sitting alone in her cherry tree, daydreaming.

"She's the best dancer I've ever seen!" Wild Cherry said out loud, swinging herself down to one of the lower branches where she often did her thinking and there was a good view of the woodland floor.

Pansy was a new arrival in Flower
Fairyland, and everyone was talking about
how her flowers had cheered up the garden
after the long, hard winter, blooming in
several brilliant colors. Wild Cherry had
seen her for the first time at the ball and
thought she was stunning. But it wasn't just
her bright dress—of purple, cream, and blue
with a loud splash of yellow—that caught the
Tree Fairy's eye, or her petal-shaped wings
in the same wonderful colors, or even her
mass of springy golden curls. It was Pansy's
confidence that truly made her sparkle.

When she talked, she was bubbly and full of life—and when she danced . . . she shone brighter than any of the stars that twinkled in the night sky.

She didn't put a foot wrong, Wild Cherry thought to herself as she picked a clump of blossom and began to absentmindedly pluck the petals one by one. *If I knew all the steps, then I wouldn't be scared to dance in front of everyone, either.* She was sitting cross-legged, and as she let the petals fall into her skirt, she began to feel a little sad.

Wild Cherry remembered how, like all
the Flower Fairies, she had learned to dance
when she was very young. She'd loved it from
the start and had practiced like mad every
night before she went to bed. However, being
a Tree Fairy, she also had climbing lessons,
and one day, when she lost her balance and
fell awkwardly, she'd injured a wing. Much
to her dismay, it meant that she couldn't
dance until it had completely healed, and
so she missed a whole series of classes where
the other fairies learned new steps.

Wild Cherry sighed for the second time that morning. *If only I wasn't so silly and shy,* she thought, scolding herself.

She knew very well that she should have asked for extra help when she'd recovered. But instead, she hid at the back of the class, struggling to keep up. And after that, although she never stopped dreaming about spinning her way around the dance floor, she wasn't brave enough to try.

The Tree Fairy shook her head to dismiss the thought and began looking for a leaf large enough to wrap up the petals she'd collected.

Just then, a flash of bright red caught her eye.

"A ladybug—to cheer me up!" Wild Cherry exclaimed.

It was quite unusual to set eyes on one so early in the year, as they like to sleep until the summer months, and in Flower Fairyland it was considered very lucky.

At that moment, the pretty beetle landed close enough for Wild Cherry to see each of its shiny black spots, and she swiftly counted them, holding her breath in anticipation.

"Seven!" she cried out in delight. Seven spots entitled you to a wish! But you had to make it before the ladybug flew away.

Quick, quick, Wild Cherry thought to herself as the ladybug spread its wings.

She squeezed her eyes shut, knowing precisely what she wanted more than anything. "I wish . . ." she said eagerly. "I wish . . . I wish I could learn to dance like Pansy!" And then she opened them at the precise moment that the ladybug launched itself into the air—whisking her wish away with it.

Chapter Two
The Dance Class

Pear Blossom was always cheerful. And
he was always full of song. Wild Cherry
loved spending the afternoon sitting in
his tree listening as he chattered away to
the garden birds. He could imitate each of
their melodies perfectly, and his treetop
was always busy with a chaffinch or thrush
bringing their young to visit him or stopping
by to catch up on Flower
Fairy news.

Wild Cherry also felt incredibly at home
surrounded by the clouds of white pear
blossom, and she often found herself talking
about things that she never told anyone else.
Soon after the last chaffinch had flown off
to find some worms for his tea, the two Tree
Fairies began to discuss the Spring Ball, and
it wasn't long before Wild Cherry had shared
her secret.

"You know, I've never noticed that you
don't actually dance at the seasonal balls!"
Pear Blossom sounded amazed. "I thought
that was practically *all* you did!"

"No," replied Wild Cherry, her cheeks tinged pink. "I just spend all my time by the dance floor *watching*."

"Well," said Pear, in a good-natured way, "we can soon change that."

Without another word, he jumped from his perch and, beckoning to his friend to follow him, flew down to the very lowest bough of the pear tree. Once there, he sat astride a branch and waited until Wild Cherry landed next to him. She was about to ask him what they were doing when he held up one hand to silence her and then cupped the other behind his pointy, elflike ear.

"Ah, good, just as I thought," Pear Blossom said, suddenly leaning right forward so that his head disappeared through the foliage.

Wild Cherry Blossom was puzzled by her friend's behaviour, but she sat still and listened intently. And then, there it was – the sound of Flower Fairies singing. Gradually, it got louder until she could quite clearly hear the words:

> "Lavender's blue, dilly dilly,
> Lavender's green;
> When you are king, dilly dilly,
> I shall be queen."

It was one of her favorite songs, and as she peered down to find out where it was coming from, the two Crocus Fairies, followed by Daffodil, Candytuft, and Tulip, came into view—waving Canterbury bells, and dancing as they sang. Or rather, they were trying to dance as best they could, but mainly they were skipping along. They were obviously enjoying themselves, though, and didn't seem remotely self-conscious. As they linked hands and formed a circle around the trunk of the pear tree, a solo voice could be heard singing the rest of the verse:

> "Who told you so, dilly dilly,
> Who told you so?
> 'Twas my own heart, dilly dilly,
> That told me so."

As the dancers joined in the chorus, out

from behind the rockery came an older
Flower Fairy moving in time to the music
with grace and ease. It was Pansy!

Pear Blossom sat upright and beamed at
Wild Cherry. "I thought it was the right time
of day for Pansy's dance lesson. You must
join in, of course!"

Then, much
to Wild Cherry's
horror, before she
could stop him,
he called, "Pansy!
Pansy! We're up here!"

The song had ended,
and his voice rang out, causing
the Garden Fairy to look up and wave.

"Oh, P-Pear ..." Wild Cherry Blossom
stuttered. "I couldn't possibly—"

But it was too late. Pansy was turning away
from her class, and it was obvious that she
was about to come and join the Tree Fairies to
find out what Pear Blossom wanted.

The Woodland Fairy was suddenly
overwhelmed by shyness. It wasn't that she
didn't want to make friends with Pansy ...
she just felt very foolish that she'd spent all
this time wishing she could dance and hiding

the fact that she couldn't.

"Afternoon, Pansy," Pear Blossom said warmly as the Garden Fairy took off from the ground. "This is my friend Wild Cherry." Pansy smiled broadly as she came to rest beside them. "And what an afternoon it's been! I was so busy looking after my flowers that I nearly forgot the time and so had to rush to my dance class." She burbled away, not in the least bit timid. "Phew—I'm really thirsty. How about making us a cup of chamomile tea?"

"No problem at all," Pear Blossom replied,

getting up. "Oh, and while I'm gone, Wild Cherry has got something to ask you."

"Go on," said Pansy, fixing her with a steady gaze.

Wild Cherry blushed fiercely. Her throat was really dry, and she felt sure that she wouldn't be able to utter a single word. Without meaning to, she panicked, and before she knew what she was saying, she squeaked, "I've got to go!"

Then she jumped to her feet and, forgetting the wish that she had made earlier that day, headed for home just as fast as her wings would carry her.

Chapter Three
Visiting

Wild Cherry Blossom had barely slept
a wink. She was so ashamed of herself for
having flown off like that. What *would* Pansy
think—and poor old Pear, who was only
trying to be kind?

*I was rude and ungrateful and not at all as a
Flower Fairy should be!* she thought to herself
as she fluttered over the garden wall.

When Wild Cherry had finally given up

trying to get any more rest, she had decided
to go and apologize to Pansy straight after
breakfast. She'd been too nervous to eat more
than a handful of dried berries, but it was a
beautiful day, and the sight of the clear blue
sky gave her energy.

It was some distance from the woodland to
the garden, and the Tree Fairy's wings were
quite sore from her frantic flight the day
before, so Wild Cherry started walking just
as soon as she could. She guessed that Pansy's
patch would be where the bravest Garden
Fairies tended to live—in the flowerbed that

bordered the human's lawn—and set off in that direction.

As she went, she reminded herself just how important manners were and that this time, when she came across the confident Garden Fairy, she would just have to overcome her shyness. *Anyway, she seemed very friendly—and she might not have thought what I did was as bad as all that.*

She was busily telling herself this as she made her way toward the front of the flowerbed and so got a tremendous shock when she parted the long thin grape hyacinth leaves. There, just a stone's throw away, was Pansy, standing boldly on the edge of the lawn talking

loudly to Dandelion. Wild Cherry's heart immediately began to beat faster.

The Tree Fairy already knew Dandelion well enough. He was full of mischief, and an impish smile never left his lips. In fact, everything about his appearance was lively. The sleeves of his tunic and his shorts were cheerful stripes of gold and green—the same color as his wings—and he had playful pompoms on his shoes.

"So how was your afternoon? Did your

class go well?" he was asking Pansy. He hopped from foot to foot as he spoke, as if he found it difficult to stay still for more than a moment. Dandelion was also an enthusiastic dancer.

"Oh, it was great!" Pansy replied. "But a strange thing happened afterwards."

Wild Cherry Blossom's heart missed a beat.

"Pear was watching, and he had a friend of his with him —Wild Cherry.'

She's going to tell him what happened and how strangely I behaved, the Tree Fairy thought to herself. *I just can't bear it!*

"Go on," said Dandelion, sounding intrigued.

Suddenly, making friends was the last

thing on Wild Cherry's mind. She felt so embarrassed! At that moment, all she wanted was to be in her own private spot in the woodlands. So, without waiting to hear what Pansy actually had to say, she scurried back the way she had come, not stopping to talk to anyone on the way.

* * *

Wild Cherry Blossom would probably
have spent the rest of the day sitting in her
tree, thinking. Although deep down she
was very disappointed with how things had
turned out, she was trying to convince herself
that it was probably for the best.

"After all, I don't even know if I can dance,
anymore," she said out loud. "At least this
way there's still hope. I mean, just imagine
if I found out that I was terrible at it—then I
couldn't even dream about being a dancer!"

Once she'd reached this conclusion, she

began to feel a bit better. So much so, that
when Bluebell called up to her to ask if she
was going out in the fields that afternoon and
if she could take a message to Heart's-ease
for him, she agreed.

When Bluebell's flowers blossomed, they

spread out like a huge carpet across the
woodland floor. So he was kept very busy
tending to them and could always be found
somewhere among their nodding blue heads.
Knowing this, the thrushes would often use
him as a drop-off point for messages that

they were delivering from the garden. Then either the Wild Flower Fairies would come and ask if he had any letters for them or he would beg a favor from a passing fairy to take them farther afield.

Wild Cherry's mood was much lighter as she made her way along a deep rut in the field where Heart's-ease lived. She soon spotted him sitting cross-legged on the freshly plowed earth, scribbling away in his notebook. He, too, was a solitary kind of fairy who spent a lot of time with his head buried in a book—either reading or filling a diary with his thoughts. Unlike Wild Cherry, though, he rarely ventured to the garden and mainly caught up on the goings-on from those that visited his corner of Flower Fairyland.

"Hello, Heart's-ease," Wild Cherry called. "I hope I'm not disturbing you."

The Wild Flower Fairy looked up.

"My dear friend! Not at all!"

Heart's-ease put down his quill pen and

indicated for Wild Cherry to sit down next to him. "So what brings you this way? It's been ages."

"I know—but it's great to see you." The Tree Fairy felt very affectionately toward Heart's-ease, as they had a lot in common.

"Can I get you a drink—jasmine tea, perhaps?" he asked her.

"Oh yes, please," she replied. Then, remembering the letter she was carrying,

Wild Cherry held it out. "This is for you from the garden—Bluebell asked me to deliver it."

Heart's-ease, who clearly didn't receive many letters, forgot all about their drinks and eagerly broke the seal on the folded sycamore leaf.

"Well, I never!" he exclaimed. "What an afternoon this is turning out to be. First of all the pleasure of your company, then an unexpected letter—and now, a very special fairy arriving for tea!"

"How lovely," Wild Cherry said sincerely, wondering who the surprise visit was from.

Judging by her friend's enthusiasm, she guessed it might be Queen of the Meadows or even Kingcup.

"Oh, Wild Cherry—I'm ever so pleased. It's my cousin from the garden, who I've never yet met. She's coming out here to see me!"

Heart's-ease was now dashing back and forth—picking up his notebook one minute, organizing tea things the next. and getting himself in quite a fluster. The Tree Fairy was gently amused. She had never seen him in such a state—ordinarily he was very calm and never in a hurry. His curly hair seemed to have taken on a life of its own, and the more he pushed it out of his eyes or tried to smooth it back, the more wiry and troublesome it became. Heart's-ease did look funny with it standing up from his head! Suppressing a giggle, Wild Cherry decided that she should lend a hand.

"I'll help you get ready, Heart's-ease. Now

tell me precisely—who is coming to tea?"

Heart's-ease stopped what he was doing and took a couple of deep breaths. "Oh, it's marvelous, Wild Cherry. She's only just arrived in Flower Fairyland. And of course, you *must* join us. I'd love you to meet my cousin."

"But you haven't told me who she is!" Wild Cherry laughed.

"Silly me." The Wild Flower Fairy grinned. "Why—it's Pansy, of course!"

Chapter Four
Faraway Friends

They couldn't be more different, Wild Cherry Blossom thought to herself.

Pansy's dress was a bold statement, whereas Heart's-ease's clothes were a more delicate design, and his wings were made up of intricate patterns as opposed to the vibrant splashes of color on hers. It seemed that the Garden Fairy was always chirpy and energetic in contrast to the Wild Fairy who preferred to be quiet and still.

But they get along really well. Wild Cherry mulled this over as she watched the two cousins, talking and laughing and having a splendid time.

When she'd discovered that Pansy was the mysterious visitor, the Tree Fairy hastily made her excuses to Heart's-ease —mumbling something about needing to get home. However, as she said good bye to her friend, she couldn't ignore the sinking feeling in the pit of her stomach. She was well aware that the situation with Pansy was going from bad to worse, and she knew that she wouldn't be able to avoid her forever. Yet she hoped that time might work its wonders, and once the memory of the silliness of the day before had faded, then it would be much easier to approach the Garden Fairy.

Wild Cherry had just left Heart's-ease and was clambering through the hedgerow when the sound of Pansy arriving stopped her in her tracks. Staying very still, she listened as the cousins exchanged greetings before settling down to tea. She was about to set off again but instead, like a moth drawn to a light, parted the leaves at the front of the hedgerow to take another peek at Pansy.

That was where Wild Cherry was now, thinking to herself how surprising life could be—what with two fairies as different as night and day getting along so well. She didn't know how long she'd been crouching there, but as she tried for the umpteenth time to get comfortable amidst the spiky twigs, Pansy announced that it was time for her to go.

"It was brilliant to meet you, cousin," the Garden Fairy said, giving Heart's-ease a kiss on the cheek. "Now you make sure you come and visit me sometime soon."

"Oh, I will," he replied, blushing to the roots of his hair. "Good bye."

Pansy turned around to wave as she picked her way down the plowed field, and when Wild Cherry heard Heart's-ease sigh contentedly to himself, she felt very pleased for her friend. In the distance Pansy could be heard humming loudly as she walked and, curiosity getting the better of her, Wild Cherry Blossom found herself following.

Pansy was happily singing the same song as the day before, and when she reached the verse that fitted her surroundings perfectly, she whooped in delight and began to dance.

"Call up your friends, dilly, dilly,
Set them to work.
Some to the plow, dilly dilly,
Some to the fork."

Each time there was a "dilly dilly", the athletic fairy kicked up both her legs in the air, causing her to leave the ground for a split second and giggle with pleasure.

"Some to the hay, dilly dilly,
Some to thresh corn,
Whilst you and I, dilly dilly,
Keep ourselves warm."

Pansy spun round and round, her floaty dress fanning out around her. Then she skipped along for a few steps before bounding elegantly. Each time she jumped, she seemed to propel herself higher and farther forward, making it look as if it was the easiest thing in the world.

Wild Cherry was utterly absorbed—she had never seen anything so wonderful in all her life. And so when the earth began to tremble beneath her feet, she didn't take much notice. *It must be Pansy's dancing that's making the ground shake*, she thought casually.

When the performance finally came to an end, the Garden Fairy collapsed in a heap, completely breathless. It was then that it dawned on Wild Cherry—not only could she still feel the vibrations beneath her feet, but they were getting stronger. She had crept along behind Pansy, keeping just out of

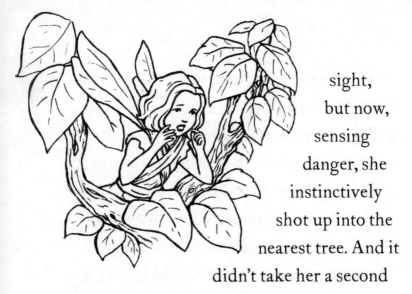

sight,
but now,
sensing
danger, she
instinctively
shot up into the
nearest tree. And it
didn't take her a second
to see what was causing the tremors.

Humans! Wild Cherry gasped, a shiver
running down her spine. *And they're coming
this way!*

She glanced down at Pansy and was
about to call out to her to fly up into
the tree when she realized that the
Garden Fairy still hadn't caught
her breath. She would never
have the strength to make the
distance and, as she wasn't a
Tree Fairy, she might not be

good enough at climbing to reach the safety of the top branches.

Boom, boom, boom! Wild Cherry's whole universe seemed to be shaking now as the children ran along in the precise direction of where Pansy was sprawled out on the path. She was in real danger of being discovered —or worse still—trampled! Wild Cherry was going to have to do something to save her, and fast!

Chapter Five
To the Rescue!

Desperate for ideas, Wild Cherry looked frantically around her.

The tree that she had flown into was an elm, and she wondered if its Flower Fairy was at home. *I dare not shout out in case the humans hear me*, she thought, quickly scanning the branches for any sign of the Flower Fairy. The leaves were dark green and would make him difficult to spot in his similarly colored clothes, unless of course he was sitting among the blossom. Wild Cherry was squinting at the tiny clusters of flowers, in a last-ditch attempt to find help, when she had a sudden flash of inspiration.

She would create a diversion! As there wasn't time to move Pansy, the only thing to do was to distract the children and lead them in a different direction. Wild Cherry rummaged around in the deep pockets of her dress—yup, she had what she needed. Taking a deep breath, she opened her wings.

"It's now or never!" she said, leaping into the air.

The two girls had slowed to a walk but were nonetheless only twenty strides or so away.

When Wild Cherry reached them, she hovered behind them and delved a hand into her pocket. Taking out a pinch of ground-up pollen, she threw it up into the air and whispered, "Fairy dust, fairy dust, bring me a breeze!"

Instantly, a warm current of wind began

to pick up. *This might just work!* the Tree
Fairy thought as she carefully unfolded
the cherry-tree leaf that she'd produced
from her other pocket. Then, plucking up
her courage, she shook the contents of the
purse at the children, getting as close as she
could without being seen. At first the white
blossom began to cascade to the ground, but
the next moment the breeze had caught the
petals, and slowly but surely they began to
dance and whirl like snowflakes.

At first, Wild Cherry thought that the girls hadn't noticed, but suddenly one of them cried out.

"Janet, look—it's snowing!" she said, coming to a halt and pointing to the flurry of blossom.

"Oh, wow!" exclaimed the shorter girl, her pretty face breaking into an enormous grin.

"Hang on a minute," her friend said, holding out an upturned hand. "These aren't snowflakes—they're petals!"

Yes! The Tree Fairy had successfully gained their interest, and so far they hadn't spotted her.

However, she knew that her job was only half done. Taking the remaining sprinkling of fairy dust from her pocket, she blew it off her hand, sending a dart of air into the midst of the swirling blossom.

After a moment or two, the petal cloud

began to move away from the children.

Wild Cherry retreated to the safety of a nearby tree and held her breath. Then, as she had hoped, the two mesmerized girls began to chase after the cloud—on a completely different course than the one that led back to Pansy's home.

* * *

"I did it, I actually did it!"

If Wild Cherry Blossom had even an ounce of energy left, she would have jumped for joy.

Five minutes or so had passed since she'd watched the children disappear into the distance, and they were no longer visible on the horizon. By the time Wild Cherry had flown into the uppermost branches to hide, there was no sign of Pansy. She just couldn't believe how well things had turned out. In fact, she couldn't remember the last time she'd felt such a thrill of success.

The sun was beginning to set, and the Tree Fairy gazed at the rich oranges and yellows melting across the afternoon sky. What a view it was from the giddy heights of a tall elm! She chuckled to herself. *There was a time when I was too scared to sit at the top of a tree*, she recalled.

It was true—not so long ago she had been a nervous climber, until the day that baby

Apple Blossom scrambled up too high and needed rescuing. Wild Cherry scratched her head. *That's twice now that I've been unexpectedly brave.*

She sat very still for a minute, lost in thought.

"On both occasions," she said aloud, "rather than worrying that I might fail, I just did something without thinking and it turned out all right."

All of a sudden the Tree Fairy got up from her resting place. "There's just one more thing I'd like to do while I remember how this feels." And summoning her remaining strength, she launched herself purposefully into the air.

Chapter Five
Hooray for Wild Cherry

Wild Cherry was concentrating so hard on carefully lowering herself down the garden wall that she hadn't heard the commotion behind her.

I don't think I've ever felt so tired, she thought to herself, her eyelids drooping. It had been a long day for the Tree Fairy, and she yearned to be tucked up in her tree. Not only had she survived on very little sleep, but it had been such an eventful day!

The energy that she'd felt when she first left the elm tree had been used up by the sheer effort of keeping herself in the air. Long before she reached the garden, her wings had given up, and now she was faced with the strenuous task of climbing down the wall.

Clap, clap, clap, clap!

"Okay. Right foot, left arm, left foot, right arm," Wild Cherry instructed herself as she went. "Nearly there now..."

Clap, clap, clap, clap!

"What on earth is that?" she wondered aloud, but didn't dare look around for fear of losing her balance.

A moment later her feet touched the ground and she immediately swung around to see where the strange noise was coming from.

Wild Cherry got such a jolt from the sight

that met her eyes that she nearly fell over.

For there, standing in a semicircle and all clapping rhythmically, were Pear Blossom, Dandelion, Zinnia, Tulip, and Pansy! And before she could utter a single word, Pear Blossom stepped forward.

"Three cheers for Wild Cherry Blossom. Hip hip hooray!" shouted her old friend, and the others joined in.

"Hip hip hooray! Hip hip hooray!"

"W-what's going on?" she asked, feeling quite dazed and utterly confused.

"I was up at the top of my tree . . . and I saw what you did . . . you were so brave! I mean to say, I know that you saved Pansy. We all do!" the words tumbled out of Pear.

Wild Cherry stared down at her shoes to avoid his eyes. All the Garden Fairies were talking at once now, but she was busy trying to stop her cheeks from burning with embarrassment. Then one voice spoke, clear above the others.

"Thank you, so much."

It was Pansy!

Wild Cherry gulped. And then, the resolve that she'd felt earlier came back to her and she looked up and met Pansy's gaze.

"I'm sorry about yesterday," she said, talking slowly so as not to stutter. "It wasn't that I didn't want to be friends with you—" She took a deep breath. "It's just that I'm shy."

"Oh, don't worry." Pansy beamed at her. "I was telling Dandelion all about it—only because I was worried that I'd done something wrong—and he explained that you can be a bit quiet sometimes."

So she didn't think I was awful! Wild Cherry breathed a sigh of relief. It had just been a ridiculous misunderstanding.

"Actually," the Tree Fairy said, suddenly not feeling in the least bit nervous, "I wanted to ask you something." And she glanced at Pear Blossom, who gave her a knowing grin and, without further ado, ushered the others away.

"Will you let me go first?" Pansy asked,
putting an arm around her shoulder and
leading her over to a couple of mushroom
stools.

Wild Cherry nodded, at the same time
gratefully sinking into the cushioned seat.

"Well," said the Garden Fairy, "you
really got me out of a sticky situation this
afternoon. So, I want to thank you. Is there
anything—anything at all—that I can do to
repay you?"

"I can't dance!" Wild Cherry blurted out.
"And I want to learn—only I'm scared that I
might not be any good at it."

Pansy chuckled. "Don't be silly! Of course you would. Anyway, that's what dance classes are for! I mean, you saw Daff and Tulip and the rest of them—they're not experts yet, but they're learning, and they're really enjoying themselves."

It was true—none of them had looked brilliant, but they were obviously eager to learn. Wild Cherry suddenly realized that she wasn't the only Flower Fairy who needed some practice. She had nothing to worry about after all.

"Besides—you're not short of courage,"
the Garden Fairy went on. "What you did to
distract those children was really brave!"

Wild Cherry smiled. "I guess so."

"I've got it!" Pansy announced, looking
pleased with herself. "What I'll do to repay
you is give you some private lessons. And
by the time the Summer Ball comes along,
you'll be one of the best dancers in Flower
Fairyland."

"Now, I won't take no for an answer." She leaned across and patted Wild Cherry kindly on the arm. "Listen, it's getting late, and I for one am starving. Come on. Pear Blossom has invited us all to supper. Race you there!"

Pansy winked at her, and Wild Cherry found herself blushing—but this time it was with pleasure.

Then, without another word, the energetic Garden Fairy sprang up from her seat and sped off.

Wild Cherry Blossom hung back for a moment and stared up at the dusky sky, trying to absorb everything that had just happened. Her wish had been granted! Finally, she would be able to dance at the fairy court. She twirled around, her arms outstretched.

"Thank you, ladybug—wherever you are!" she called into the darkness, and then, forgetting her tiredness, she skipped and danced to catch up with her new friend.

FLOWER FAIRIES™ FRIENDS

Visit our Flower Fairies website at:

www.flowerfairies.com

There are lots of fun Flower Fairy games and activities for you to play, plus you can find out more about all your favorite fairy friends!

Have you logged onto the Flower Fairies™ Friends Friendship Ring?

In the land of Fairyopolis every fairy is your friend
and now the Flower Fairies
want to share their secrets with you!

No Membership Fee

Online Fun

Visit **www.flowerfairies.com**
and sign up for the Flower
Fairies Friendship Ring
and you will receive:

✿ Secret Fairy Coded Messages
✿ News and updates
✿ Invitations to special events
✿ Every new friend receives a
special gift from the Flower Fairies!
(while supplies last.)

Frederick Warne & Co.
A division of Penguin Young Readers Group

This book
belongs to

....

To my sister, Emma

FREDERICK WARNE

Published by the Penguin Group
Penguin Books Ltd, 80 Strand, London WC2R 0RL, England
Penguin Young Readers Group, 345 Hudson Street,
New York, New York 10014, U.S.A.
Penguin Books Australia Ltd, 250 Camberwell Road, Camberwell,
Victoria 3124, Australia
Canada, India, New Zealand, South Africa

2

Copyright © Frederick Warne & Co., 2007

New reproductions of Cicely Mary Barker's illustrations
copyright © The Estate of Cicely Mary Barker, 1990
Original text and illustrations copyright
© The Estate of Cicely Mary Barker,
1923, 1925, 1926, 1934, 1940, 1944, 1948

All rights reserved

ISBN: 978 0 7232 5951 0

Printed in Great Britain

Poppy's Perfect Home

By Pippa Le Quesne

Welcome to the Flower Fairies' Garden!

Where are the fairies?
Where can we find them?
We've seen the fairy-rings
They leave behind them!

Is it a secret
No one is telling?
Why, in your garden
Surely they're dwelling!

No need for journeying,
Seeking afar:
Where there are flowers,
There fairies are!

Contents

Chapter One
Terrible News

Poppy carefully cupped the sticky mixture first in one hand and then the other. She rolled it clockwise and then turned it over and rolled it again until she had gently shaped it into a small sphere. Then she popped it at the end of a row of balls that were lined up on a leaf in the baking sun.

"Perfect!" Poppy said, wiping her hands on the faded pink apron that she always wore when she was cooking. She'd had the apron for as long as she could remember and it had been washed so many times that it was quite thin in places. But it had been a present from her friend Tansy and the Flower Fairy firmly believed that it brought her good luck.

"Now, I definitely deserve a cup of tea," she thought out loud, feeling very pleased with the number of leaves lying on the

ground all around her. They were covered in clusters of nectar-coated poppy seeds, which were turning deliciously brittle in the heat.

It had been a hot, clear day, and Poppy had worked hard. The moon was due to be full in a few days' time and she needed to make a large batch of popcorn ready for her stall at the Fairy Fair. It was a special market that took place in a secret glade in the woods, once a month on the night of the full moon. There was music and dancing, delicious things to eat and the promise of a royal appearance from Kingcup and the Queen of the Meadow. Ever since Poppy had been old enough to attend, she hadn't missed a single one.

She had just untied her apron and was shaking some wayward seeds from the folds of her bright red dress, when she heard the sound of urgent voices.

"Poppy!
Are you
there?"
"Poppy—
where are you?"
"I'm here," she
replied, leaping in
the air and beating
her wings at the same
time so that a moment later
she was hovering just above the
leafy patch. Scanning the meadow, she saw
a flash of yellow in the long grass, followed
immediately by another, and then she caught
sight of two of the younger Flower Fairies,
running in her direction.

"Buttercup, Cowslip—over here!" Poppy
called cheerfully, feeling glad to have some
company now that she had finished her
chores. But when they turned their faces

towards her, her heart missed a beat . . . For instead of greeting her with their usual broad grins, the look on their faces was one of pure panic. Something was wrong. Terribly wrong.

"And you heard it from the elves?" Poppy breathed a sigh of relief. "Well, that makes me feel a lot better—it's bound to be one of their mischievous schemes to cause havoc in Flower Fairyland."

She smiled kindly at her two guests, who had cooled off after a glass of elderflower juice, but were still upset. Cowslip was shaking her head. "I know what you mean, Poppy, but these elves have been living in the hedgerow between our meadow and yours all summer, and they consider it home now. And today they were frantically packing and looked more flustered than I've ever seen them. They said they were moving straight back to the marsh—permanently."

Buttercup nodded in agreement. "It's definitely not one of their pranks. And they told us that they'd heard it from some of the fairies who live close to the farm—Ragwort and Ground Ivy—so you could always check with them." She gazed seriously at Poppy. "What are you going to do?"

"Well, if you're positive about this, then I'll call a meadow meeting right away. Now, the most helpful thing that you two can do is to go back to your side of the hedgerow and listen out for any more news. And double check that you're all safe over there, will you?" The older Flower Fairy got to her feet and, tying her apron in such a way so that it

acted as a sling, she began tipping each of the
leaves into it. Then she filled her two friends'
pockets with some of the mouth-watering
popcorn. "Thank you for coming so quickly,"
she said, kissing them both on their cheeks.

"Bye," Cowslip murmured. "And—we're
sorry to bring you such awful news," she
added.

"Don't worry," Poppy replied lightly. "There's bound to be a simple solution."

"Let us know what you decide, won't you?" Buttercup said, looking unusually serious.

"I will, of course." Poppy tried to sound as bright as possible as they exchanged goodbyes but, as she watched them flit away, she couldn't help herself from clutching her lucky apron and whispering, "Although I do hope you're wrong." Then she hurried off in the opposite direction, keen to find her meadow companions as quickly as possible.

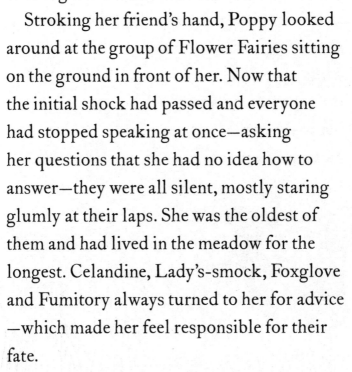

* * *

Celandine was sobbing into her handkerchief. "W-w-we're d-d-doomed!" she stuttered, choking back a fresh wave of tears.

Stroking her friend's hand, Poppy looked around at the group of Flower Fairies sitting on the ground in front of her. Now that the initial shock had passed and everyone had stopped speaking at once—asking her questions that she had no idea how to answer—they were all silent, mostly staring glumly at their laps. She was the oldest of them and had lived in the meadow for the longest. Celandine, Lady's-smock, Foxglove and Fumitory always turned to her for advice —which made her feel responsible for their fate.

Yet, she had never been faced with such a

big problem or one that didn't seem to have a straightforward answer. She needed some time to think, and on her own. Clearing her throat, she tried to look confident.

"It's ok, leave it to me. Everyone go home and get a good night's rest and meet me back here first thing in the morning," she said reassuringly. "You don't need to be sad—I'll work something out."

"Thanks," said Foxglove, in a brave voice. "We can always count on you."

Poppy smiled and gave each one of them an encouraging pat or a hug as they left. But once they were all out of sight, the tall slender Flower Fairy crumpled back to the ground and buried her head in her arms.

"This can't be happening!" she cried. "How could anyone want to destroy our beautiful home?"

A Welcome Visit

Breaking the terrible news to her friends had been the worst moment of her life. Buttercup and Cowslip had told Poppy that humans had bought the field and were planning to plough it up and replant it for farming. The fairies that lived there had always considered themselves lucky—other than the occasional group of ramblers stopping for a picnic, their peaceful existence was rarely disturbed by humans.

And now we're going to be homeless. Poppy gulped. In her right hand she held one of the strong stems of her plant. Its papery scarlet petals and intense black face towered above her.

What would happen to all of their flowers? *I've got to think of something. Everyone's depending on me*, she told herself.

Although her small chin trembled with sadness, her black wings with their jagged red edges stood proud from her back. Taking one final look and wiping away the last of her tears, she settled herself down on the hillock and prepared herself for a long night of thinking.

"Poppy?"

"Hmm?" The Flower Fairy had been deep in thought and hadn't noticed the starling landing lightly in front of her. She beamed when she recognized her friend.

Poppy could understand and talk to all

of the birds, but the starling that visited her meadow to catch grubs was her favorite by far. He was so chatty and he could never stay still for long, darting along the ground or hopping on the spot, adding a trill or a warble into his sentences as he relayed some interesting bit of gossip.

"Why the miserable face?"

"How long have you got?" Poppy sighed.

It was nearly dawn now and although she'd been thinking hard all night, she hadn't come up with any good ideas. Initially, she

had thought that if all the Flower Fairies collected together their fairy dust, they might be able to cast a spell powerful enough to protect the meadow. But it didn't take her

long to realize that it would be impossible to keep it going *forever* as their spells weren't very strong or permanent. The Flower Fairies made the magic dust from each of their individual flowers and they used it when they needed a helping hand in a tricky situation. However, this was more of a crisis and it needed a lot more than a helping hand...

"I've always time for you," the starling was

saying. "I'll give my feathers a preen while I'm listening."

So while he busily primped and tweaked with his pointed beak, Poppy told him all about her problem.

"Why can't you just move to the next meadow where Buttercup and Cowslip live?" the starling asked, when she'd finished.

"Well, we could," the Flower Fairy explained. "But—and I'm sure this won't happen—if we sow all our seeds there and then the farmer bought that field too and we had to move again before our flowers had grown . . . or if they didn't grow successfully. . ." Poppy blinked back the tears that were pricking her eyes. "Well, that would be it. Our flowers would become extinct."

"Oh, how dreadful! I hadn't thought of that." The starling trilled in alarm. "If there's

anything I can do, you know I'll help?"

"Yes, I know, you're a dear." Poppy smiled in appreciation. "Now, listen, it's wonderful to see you but I've got to come up with something in the next couple of hours, so it's probably best if I'm on my own."

"Absolutely, I understand,' he replied cheerfully, smoothing down his glossy feathers. "Oh, before I forget—I was in the Flower Fairies' Garden yesterday and saw our old friend Primrose. She sends her love." And the bird dipped his beak in farewell and took to the air.

"Thanks!" called Poppy, watching him fly away, his wings flashing purple and green in the morning sunlight. As he disappeared on the horizon, she thought how nice it must be to be able to make your home in any tree that you chose, knowing that you could fly any distance to forage for food. Or being able to travel a long way very quickly to visit friends far and wide. It took her the best part of a day to reach the Flower Fairies' Garden and the effort was exhausting.

"Oh, my," Poppy said slowly, as something that the starling had mentioned sank in. "That's it!" An idea had suddenly popped into her head, and although it might take some careful planning, it could definitely work . . .

Chapter Three
A Hasty Departure

"So ... So, we'd have to literally abandon our plants and make our way to the garden in the hope of finding a new patch?" Foxglove looked unhappily at Poppy. "I mean—obviously I'm incredibly grateful that you've come up with a plan and it's a great idea. It's just such a shock ..."

Foxglove was one of the most striking Flower Fairies that Poppy knew. He was clothed almost entirely in dark purple—

from the tip of his sharp-pointed shoes
right to the hood that his impish face and
angular ears poked out from. Only his jaunty
shorts weren't purple. They were gold with
burgundy spots, like the speckled insides of
his flowers. His flowers hung in bells from
a spike rising way above the Flower Fairy's
head. His plants were also one of the most
noticeable features of the meadow—the lofty
blooms visible all around the perimeter. And
Foxglove could often be found climbing
up one to get a better view or to exchange
news with the bumble bees while they were
collecting pollen.

He was such a happy, outgoing fellow
that seeing him looking so downhearted was
especially upsetting.

"I know," Poppy said gently. "It's almost
unbearable to think of. But we've so many
friends in the garden—and I've sent the

starling ahead to ask if there might be an area
large enough for us all to stay together. So
we'd still have each other."

"You're very thoughtful, Poppy." Fumitory
made this comment, but there was a general
murmur of agreement from all assembled.
"However," she went on, "I think it's best if
I stay put." Celandine opened her mouth in
surprise but shut it again when Fumitory
continued talking. "My plants have never

25

ever grown in the garden and as much as I would like to get to know the Flower Fairies that live there, I'm going to take my chances in Buttercup and Cowslip's meadow."

"But, it's a risk—as I explained earlier." Poppy frowned.

"I know," replied Fumitory. "But I'm more afraid that if I grow my plants in the garden then the humans will find them and, not recognizing them, will think they're weeds

and pull them out."

Celandine gasped, and seeing that she looked a bit faint, Poppy put a supportive arm around her. She glanced at the others—Lady's-smock and Foxglove appeared to be confused and she guessed that they were trying to decide which move would be for the best.

"Listen," she said. "I know what you're saying, dear Fumitory, but you've heard of

the Country Queen, haven't you?" All of
her listeners nodded to show that they had.
"Well—I'm old enough to remember when
she lived in this very meadow. Of course, she
loved it in the wild, but she knew many of the
Garden Flower Fairies and felt very at home
among them. So much so that, one day, she
decided to go and live there."

"And was she happy?" asked Lady's-
smock.

"She still is," Poppy said, with a twinkle in
her eye, "but she has a new name. I'm talking

about Primrose!"

"Primrose was the Country Queen?!" exclaimed Foxglove. "I never would have guessed. I must say that I've always been amazed at how much she knows about the meadow. But she seems, er . . . tamer than us somehow, as though all she has ever known is a more ordered life."

Poppy chuckled. "There are all sorts of *different* kinds of fairies that live in the Flower Fairies' Garden. And yes, Primrose is very organized —which

is why she likes it there—but wait until you get to know Dandelion and Sycamore!" She turned to Fumitory. "So, what do you think?"

But before Fumitory could answer, there was a sudden deafening roar of an engine, and all of the Flower Fairies shot into the nearest hedgerow, fleeing for cover.

"Gather your fairy dust and any seeds that you might have stored—and let's go!"

Poppy was trying hard not to tremble as she issued orders to her frightened friends.

Once she was sure that whatever was making the unearthly noise wasn't too close

by, she'd sent Foxglove up one of his plants to see what was going on. He'd come back, ashen-faced and shaking.

"It's—it's happening already," he'd reported, his eyes wide with fear.

"What is, Foxglove? What did you see?" Lady's-smock had asked, jumping up and down impatiently.

"A big blue tractor with the most horrific thing attached to the back of it. It was huge and metal and had lots of sharp bits on it and ...and..."

"Take a deep breath. It's all right," Poppy had told him, although her heart was in her mouth—for she knew what he was describing was a *plough*.

"And it's ripping out the grass at the bottom of the meadow and throwing up great chunks of soil!" Foxglove gushed and then he collapsed in a heap on the ground, too upset to say anything else.

So, she'd taken a couple of deep breaths herself and then set about thinking what needed doing in the minutes that were left before they were in *real* danger.

Now, her meadow companions stood before her—each with a basket or a knapsack holding a few belongings. Poppy had put her essential possessions in her apron first thing that morning, and it hung across one shoulder, still tied as a sling. The grinding

and crashing of the machinery was now much nearer and the entire world seemed to be shaking and juddering around them.

"Obviously, we have no choice but to leave —and fast," Poppy said. "There's no time to make a proper plan now, so let's just get over to the next meadow and we'll make a decision then."

"I can't bear to even *hear* those monstrous machines," wailed Celandine, her pale green wings drooping.

"Don't worry," Poppy replied. "We're going to get far away very soon. But first things first—we need to put the hedgerow between us and the humans so that we're safe."

The other Flower Fairies nodded sadly and then, one by one, each with a forlorn backward glance at their fast-disappearing home, they reluctantly pushed their way

through the hedge.

Poppy was the final one to go. She took one last, desperate look at her vibrant flowers— swaying serenely in the breeze—and then, swallowing a painful lump in her throat, fled after her friends.

Chapter Four
A New Beginning

After an initial dash to put some distance between themselves and the hedgerow, the evacuees congregated at the top end of the neighboring meadow. Now they were sitting with Buttercup, who was doing her best to comfort them—having made cups of tea and offered them somewhere to sleep that night. Only Fumitory had accepted. With her head bowed, the little wild fairy asked

Buttercup if she might, in fact, stay with her on a semi-permanent basis while she sowed some seeds and waited for new plants to grow. She managed a half-smile when her friend warmly welcomed her to the patch, but Poppy could see how painful it was for her to watch the rest of them depart.

"Thanks for the offer, Buttercup, but we have to keep going. None of us can bear to be anywhere near the meadow while it's being destroyed." Poppy swallowed hard. Despite all that had happened and the fact that she was surviving on only an hour's sleep, she managed to fight back the tears. She had to stay strong for the other Flower Fairies. They still had a long way to go and someone had to take command.

"Listen," Buttercup said. "The humans are probably going to be driving back and forth all day on the lane and the quickest way to the

Flower Fairies' Garden is to cross it. Now, I know that they're busy with this horrible ploughing business," she said this last bit in a respectfully hushed voice, "but humans are never too busy to ignore the sight of fairies ... It's just too risky—"

"I know, Buttercup, and we'll do everything we can to make sure they don't spot us," Poppy interrupted, only too aware that they would be putting Flower Fairyland in peril if any of the

farm laborers caught sight of them.

"Wait." Buttercup held up a hand. "I was going to say, let me sprinkle some fairy dust on you all just as you leave—and with the right spell it'll act as an invisible mantle and get you safely across. You'll have to be quick as it'll be spread quite thinly among you—but it should work."

Poppy gratefully agreed on behalf of the others and she could see the look of relief on Lady's-smock's face. Like her flowers, Lady's-smock was pale and petite and the journey was going to be gruelling enough for her without the extra element of danger.

"OK, then, huddle close—and here, Fumitory, you take a handful too," Buttercup instructed, holding out the chestnut leaf she'd just unfolded.

"Thank you, my dears—we shall be perfectly safe because of you," Poppy said, smiling bravely at Buttercup and then Fumitory, whose eyes were brimming with unshed tears. "And we'll come back and visit you soon. Now—on the count of three—" She checked to see that Lady's-smock, Celandine and Foxglove were ready to take flight. "One . . . two . . . three!"

On her command, the two Flower Fairies threw the miniscule particles of fairy dust over them and, simultaneously, the departing friends opened their wings and took to the air.

"Fairy dust, fairy dust, hide them from view, help them fly quickly and safely too," called Buttercup.

And, as the cloud of fine powder began to twinkle and sparkle, the four fairies gradually vanished from sight, until the only clue to their whereabouts was a shimmering haze that moved swiftly over the top of the hedgerow and disappeared into the lane beyond ...

Poppy sat, hugging her knees, staring up at the stars. *They're still the same*, she thought to herself, *so not everything has changed.*

Although she was more exhausted than she could ever remember, her head was buzzing with the events of what had felt like the longest day of her life.

Despite the sudden rattling of a tractor, which had given them all a tremendous

fright, the four Flower Fairies had kept their course and made it safely across the lane before the fairy dust had worn off. Then they had flown as far as their wings could take

them before landing in the middle of the vast expanse of marsh. There, the travellers had been surprised and delighted to be met by Mallow, who had heard whisperings on the breeze that they were coming. She'd given each of them one of her special fairy cheeses, which filled their hungry stomachs and cheered them up enormously.

When it was time to start moving again,
their wings were still aching too much
to fly any further, so they set off on foot,
determined to complete their journey before
the sun set. And Cotton-Grass and Rush-
Grass—Mallow's friends, who were guides—
had offered to show them the quickest route
across the marsh to the lane on the other side.

But when Poppy and her jaded
companions bade them farewell and
watched them fly off into the
dusk, every one of them
agreed that although
it was only a short
distance to go now,
they were all too
impossibly tired
to make it.

Poppy had

just begun to seek out a suitable section of bush for them to crawl under for the night, when a rapid series of chirrups alerted her to the arrival of two starlings. And there was her dear friend, and his mate, ready to take them to the special patch that they had found—a place that the kind Garden Fairies said they could call their own!

We've been so fortunate today, Poppy thought, glancing at Foxglove, Celandine and Lady's-smock, who were sleeping peacefully, curled up on the ground around her.

It was getting dark when the two birds alighted in the bottom corner of the garden and most of the Flower Fairies were in bed, but there was Rose to greet them—with cups of chamomile tea and warm moss blankets and promises of a proper welcome the next morning.

"So this is our new . . ." Poppy couldn't

bring herself to even whisper the word. She was incredibly grateful that they had made it safely to the garden and she'd been bowled over by all the help they'd had on the way. And she knew that, given time, they'd all be very happy there, but just at that moment it was impossible to think of anywhere but the meadow as home.

Celandine sighed and turned over in her sleep and Poppy smiled to see her peaceful little face. "But we're still all together," she said softly, making herself comfortable and laying down her head for the night, "and that's the most important thing."

Chapter Five
Celebrations!

"Wake up, Poppy!
Wake up!"

Poppy groaned and
opened one eye. It was
Foxglove, looking fit to
burst about something.

"What time is it?" The sleepy
Flower Fairy sat up and stretched. It felt
very early.

"Never mind that," replied her friend
impatiently. "You've got to come and see
this!" And without further ado, Foxglove
turned on his heel and disappeared around
the back of the rose bushes.

Three whole seasons had passed since
Poppy and the others had come to live in

the garden. Rose had dedicated a corner of her secret rose garden to them and they had set about making a new home and sowing their seeds. They had dug themselves an allotment and lovingly fed and watered the soil to give their plants the best possible chance to flourish. And then they had waited.

Then, one bright spring morning, the four meadow friends were rewarded for their hard work. One of Celandine's tender green shoots pushed its way through the earth and gradually unfurled. Soon, others came to join it and the allotment was dotted with yellow stars, and it was not long before Lady's-smock's dainty mauve flowers were all around the patch too. And since the larks had hailed the start of summer, Foxglove and Poppy had anxiously awaited their turn.

"Could this be it?" Poppy said to herself, springing to her feet and hurrying over the dewy grass.

As she rounded the thorny bush, now
adorned with heavenly scented blooms,
she gasped. For there, in front of her, were
not only a dozen stunning foxgloves—
standing tall and strong—but several
clumps of her own glorious poppies,
bobbing around on their bendy stems
with their waxy red petals and
sooty faces.

"We've done it!" she yelled, flinging her arms around Foxglove, who was beaming from ear to ear. "We've done it!"

"Mmmm, mmm," mumbled Candytuft, her mouth so full of popcorn that Poppy couldn't make out what she was saying.

"I may have lost my touch," said Poppy nervously. "I mean it's practically been a year since I last made any popcorn." She looked shyly down at her old pink apron, which until now had remained folded up, unused

for just as long.

Since their flight to the garden, Poppy hadn't attended the Fairy Fair. Other than one trip back to the meadow—which had been nothing more than neatly ploughed earth and such a distressing sight that she'd resolved not to return—she hadn't really ventured into the wild. She'd also stopped going to the moonlit market because she hadn't wanted to run her popcorn stall for fear of using up her scant supply of poppy seeds in case the planted ones didn't flower. But now that *all* the meadow flowers had successfully bloomed, the four friends had decided to throw a party to celebrate and also to thank the Garden Flower Fairies for their wonderful hospitality. And, of course, a party wouldn't be complete without special treats!

"It's absolutely delicious!" announced Candytuft, swallowing the last mouthful.

"You haven't lost your touch at all." She licked her lips in appreciation. "Gosh—I really have missed your popcorn."

Poppy grinned. Candytuft was renowned for the adventurous sweet delicacies that she created, so her approval was very important.

"Excellent," Poppy said. "And thanks for your help. Right I've got work to do—we'll see you this evening just after sunset. Don't be late!"

"I won't!" promised Candytuft, skipping round the rose bush and back into the main garden.

* * *

"Foxglove, Foxglove,
What see you now?
The soft summer moonlight
On bracken, grass, and bough;
And all the fairies dancing
As only they know how."

Foxglove had flown all around the allotment, dropping glow worms into upturned flowers and tucking them into curled leaves, so that they acted as lanterns and, along with the pearly moon, bathed the secret garden in a lustrous light. Now, he was perched in one of his plants, crooning his song to an

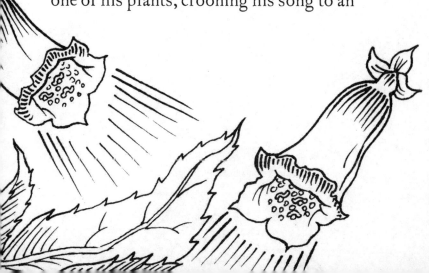

appreciative audience of Flower Fairies, who laughed and clapped at the words.

Overflowing bowls of freshly toasted popcorn nestled in the grass, and there were other goodies such as walnut and date cake, crystallized honeycomb, and rosewater punch. All the guests had arrived in their most gorgeous outfits and the scene was

spectacular. The party had only just started but the starlings were on hand to warble out tunes to accompany the dancing, and everyone appeared to be in a celebratory mood.

"You've all settled in so well," said Primrose, an arm around her friend's shoulder, "that it's hard to remember a time when you didn't live here."

Poppy nodded appreciatively. They were sitting together on a mushroom stool, soaking up the atmosphere and chatting. It was true—Foxglove had become popular for his entertaining company and when he wasn't busy in the allotment he could be found tearing through the garden with the likes of Dandelion, Sycamore and Cornflower. And Celandine and Lady's-smock had become best friends with quiet Jasmine and thoughtful Rose. She too had had a happy time—she'd enjoyed seeing more of Tansy and Primrose and she'd got to know Sweet Pea, who often dropped by with her sister and a gaggle of the baby fairies. The garden was a fantastic place to live—there was always something fun going on. But somehow, Poppy's heart still ached for meadow life. She longed to hear the crickets chirping on a warm evening, or to witness the newborn field mice first opening their eyes, or to drink the dew that had gathered overnight on the enormous leaves. She missed it all.

Primrose was giving her a knowing look. "You should go back, you know."

Poppy was jolted from her thoughts.

"I've seen that faraway look of yours." Her friend laughed. "And now you've got some more seeds, there's no real excuse."

Poppy looked at her enquiringly.

"If the feeling's there, it'll never go away. And one day, you'll wake up and think you've got too many roots here and that it's too late." Primrose slid off the mushroom and smiled. "I'm going to get a another drink" she said,

waving her cup. "Think about it!"

The nimble Flower Fairy disappeared into the throng and Poppy found herself alone. She gazed up at the stars and sighed.

Is Primrose right? she wondered. *Is it really time to go back to the wild?*

Chapter Six

The Homecoming

"Right. All set?"

Poppy nodded at Foxglove. Then she grinned at Tansy, who stood at the front of the crowd of Flower Fairies that had gathered to see her off, and patted her apron sling. "The last time I wore this, it brought us all here safely. And we may have lost the meadow that day but we gained a lot of very dear friends." She looked sheepishly round at them all. "So, I'm hoping that my lucky apron will bring me the same good fortune today and find me a new home."

"What's your plan?" Celandine said quietly, slipping her small hand into Poppy's.

"I'm going back to Buttercup and Cowslip's field to see where Fumitory has settled."

"We all wish you the best of luck," Primrose interjected. "And remember— there'll always be a home for you here."

"That's right," Rose added. "I'll make sure your poppies continue to thrive."

"Yes, we'll take care of them." Lady's-smock looked up at Poppy. "But you'll come back and visit, won't you?"

"Of course I will!" exclaimed the older Flower Fairy. "I'd miss you all too much if I didn't." Then, taking one last glance round the secret garden, which she'd grown immensely fond of, she clambered on to the back of the starling, who was waiting to carry

her off. "Farewell! I'll be back at the Fairy Fair soon, if all goes well. Enjoy the rest of the party!"

Wrapping her arms around the bird's neck, she whispered to him that she was ready to go. And as her stomach began to churn with anticipation, the starling flapped his strong wings and soon they were soaring high above the garden.

Poppy opened her eyes.

The sun was higher in the sky than when she usually woke and its warmth had stirred her from her sleep. She got up and stretched, taking huge lungfuls of country air. It felt *so*

good to be back and she couldn't remember the last time she had slept so well.

Fumitory had been just about to turn in for the night when the starling had dropped Poppy off, but she'd been thrilled to see her old friend and they'd sat up talking until their eyelids were heavy and neither of them could stay awake any longer.

"Good morning!" It was Fumitory. "I've been gathering wild strawberries."

"Oooh, lovely, I'm starved," said Poppy, thinking that all her senses seemed more acute in the wild and that she was hungrier than usual.

"Well, bring a couple with you—there's something I've been

dying to show you." replied Fumitory, producing a handkerchief from her pocket. "But it's a surprise, so I'm going to blindfold you."

"Blindfold me?!" Poppy giggled, then taking a huge bite of a sweet berry, stood still

obediently while her friend secured the petal strip over her eyes.

"Here—take my hand. We're going to fly but I'll guide you," Fumitory instructed.

So, hand in hand, flapping their gossamer wings, the two Flower Fairies took off. It was an odd sensation for Poppy—flying, but not knowing where she was heading—however she trusted her friend completely and a thrill of excitement went through her.

They hadn't covered a very large distance when Fumitory directed them back down to the ground and let go of Poppy's hand.

"Are you ready?" She began untying the handkerchief. "OK—here goes . . . Surprise!"

It took a moment for Poppy's eyes to adjust to the light but when they did, they were met by a remarkable sight. "Oh my goodness!" she said, quite simply. "But where are we?"

For they had landed at the top end of a field that was furrowed and obviously farmland. However, atop the mounds of soil, swathes of wild flowers were growing. There were clusters of Fumitory's plants—with their feathery blue-green foliage and tiny pink flowers which gave the impression of smoke billowing across the earth. And . . . Poppy couldn't believe her eyes—there were clumps of *her* resplendent scarlet flowers scattered *all over* the meadow.

"It's *our* meadow, Poppy. I don't know how it's happened, but it really is." Fumitory held out a steadying hand to her friend. "The birds tell me they've seen it happen before— varieties of flowers that are so stubborn that they'll grow anywhere—no matter what!"

"It's incredible," breathed Poppy.

"I know," replied Fumitory. "I only discovered this a few days ago—despite living so close, I've been avoiding coming here." Her face was wet with tears. "It's so good to have you back, Poppy. I didn't want to send for you as I thought you might be happy in the garden and I didn't want to make it difficult for you, but—"

"I was happy," Poppy interrupted. "But I could never *ever* be happier than here in our meadow. And just like our flowers—I'm never going to leave it."

She turned to Fumitory and squeezed her hand in appreciation. Then, feeling as though her heart would burst for joy, she whooped and set off down the meadow, shouting at the top of her voice, "We're home! We're really home!"

Visit our Flower Fairies website at:

www.flowerfairies.com

There are lots of fun Flower Fairy games and activities for you to play, plus you can find out more about all your favorite fairy friends!

Log onto the
Flower Fairies
Friendship Ring

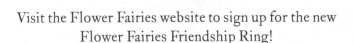

Visit the Flower Fairies website to sign up for the new Flower Fairies Friendship Ring!

★ No membership fee
★ News and updates
★ Every new friend receives a special gift!
(while supplies last)

This book
belongs to

....

For Sarah

FREDERICK WARNE

Published by the Penguin Group
Penguin Books Ltd, 80 Strand, London WC2R 0RL, England
Penguin Young Readers Group, 345 Hudson Street,
New York, New York 10014, U.S.A.
Penguin Books Australia Ltd, 250 Camberwell Road, Camberwell,
Victoria 3124, Australia
Canada, India, New Zealand, South Africa

6

Copyright © Frederick Warne & Co., 2006

New reproductions of Cicely Mary Barker's illustrations
copyright © The Estate of Cicely Mary Barker, 1990
Original text and illustrations copyright
© The Estate of Cicely Mary Barker,
1923, 1925, 1926, 1934, 1940, 1944, 1948

All rights reserved

Printed in Great Britain

Lavender's Midsummer Mix-up

by Kay Woodward

Welcome to the Flower Fairy Garden!

Where are the fairies?
Where can we find them?
We've seen the fairy-rings
They leave behind them!

Is it a secret
No one is telling?
Why, in your garden
Surely they're dwelling!

No need for journeying,
Seeking afar:
Where there are flowers,
There fairies are!

Contents

Chapter One
Party Petals

"Phew!" Lavender heaved a huge sigh of relief and flopped down on a mossy hillock. She'd had the busiest—and best—week ever, getting ready for tomorrow's Midsummer Party, and everything was nearly done.

Lavender had the strangest of hobbies. While some Flower Fairies liked to help by stirring nutshells of fairy nectar or stringing garlands of honeysuckle and forget-me-not from branch to branch and twig to twig, she was at her happiest when up to her elbows in sparkling soapsuds.

On Monday, Lavender had scurried about the Flower Fairy Garden, reminding everyone about the Midsummer Party. Then she went back to her own beautiful flower and waited below its fragrant petals.

Soon, there was a long queue of Flower Fairies lining up to see her, each clutching a dirty, crumpled outfit and wearing an anxious smile.

"Is there anything at all you can do?" asked Elder tentatively, handing over a bundle of frothy lace that looked as if it had been dipped in mud.

"Hmm…" Lavender peered closely at the

delicate frock. "It'll take a hefty sprinkling of fairy magic…" She glanced up at worried-looking Elder and smiled. "But it'll be as good as new."

"Oh, thank you," breathed the little fairy, who was just as beautiful as her dress.

Next came Sycamore, who was well known for his treetop gymnastics. Lavender wasn't surprised to see that his leafy jacket and amber shorts were ripped to shreds. Again. Sycamore winked cheekily at Lavender, who tutted and dropped his rags on top of Elder's dress.

"Next!" she said briskly, wondering where

she had put her thistle needle and dandelion thread.

By Tuesday, the teetering pile of party laundry had become taller than Lavender, and she couldn't help feeling slightly nervous about the huge task that loomed ahead. Shaking long, dark curls from her face, she collected tablets of her own special lavender soap.

Suddenly, the air filled with a snowy fluttering of wings, and Lavender looked up, first with surprise and then with delight, to see her best friends.

"You're here!" she exclaimed as the swarm of white butterflies enveloped her in a ticklish hug. Without even waiting to be asked, they zoomed toward the dirty clothes, and in seconds a very strange procession was winding its way toward the stream—first Lavender, then a bobbing row of petal bonnets, dainty shoes, and other assorted items of fairy clothing, each carried by a dazzling white butterfly.

"Thank you!" cried Lavender, as the butterflies waved good bye. She dunked the first garment into the clear water, catching a glimpse of yellow out of the corner of her eye. She knew that this was Iris, a sweet but shy fairy who lived at the water's edge.

Lavender didn't call out, knowing that Iris would venture over when she was ready.

* * *

By Wednesday, all the Flower Fairy party clothes had been rubbed and scrubbed and scrubbed and rubbed clean. And Lavender and Iris were firm friends.

"So you really, truly do *enjoy* doing this?" asked Iris, who was having great difficulty understanding the idea that Lavender did laundry for fun. Iris was a very pretty fairy. The sunlight made her glossy auburn hair look extra-shiny, while her glorious yellow dress simply shone.

Lavender shrugged dispiritedly. "I have no

choice, really," she said. "Not until the elves lift the wicked charm that binds me to a life of soap and—" Unable to keep a straight face for a second longer, she giggled loudly at Iris's horrified expression. "I don't suppose you're any good at hanging out clothes…?" she added quickly.

"Of course!" replied Iris, jumping down to the riverbank to lend a hand.

Politely, Lavender asked the spiders if they could provide the washing lines. They were happy to oblige and were soon reeling out lengths of glistening gossamer, which Lavender stretched from flower to flower. Soon, sparkling clean party petals were flapping gently on the lines.

* * *

On Thursday, instead of taking a day off while the warm breeze dried the beautiful outfits, Lavender had been busier than ever.

She realized that her stocks of lavender-scented soap were running low and that they'd be much in demand before the Midsummer Party—the one event when everyone wanted to smell extra-specially delicious.

She gathered together her ingredients: three hundred and sixty-five lavender petals, to make soap that would smell fragrant on every day of the year; a sprinkling of fairy dust, to make sure the soap made whatever it touched magically clean; and a buttercup filled to the brim with dew, to bind everything together.

Lavender dropped all of the ingredients into a beechnut shell and, using a long stem from her own flower, stirred vigorously until everything had dissolved. Then, she poured the mixture into tiny nutshell molds and left them to set. Nothing was wasted—even the leftover drops were used to make a beautiful scent for the lucky Flower Fairies to dab on their wrists.

* * *

On Friday morning, the rising sun had revealed a kaleidoscope of dazzling color. Row upon row of fine garments, made from the prettiest petals, leaves, berries, and seeds that the Flower Fairy Garden had to offer, billowed in the breeze.

"Do you know what?" said Iris thoughtfully, "if you squint a bit, you can't see the purply-red stain on Elderberry's frock at all."

Lavender was shocked. How could she have let this happen? She'd been so careful! She tore across the grass, skidding to a halt before Elderberry's spotless dress… and heard Iris giggling gleefully behind her.

"Only teasing!" called Iris, delighted to have caught Lavender out.

That'll teach me, thought Lavender with a chuckle.

And now that everything really was clean,

there was one finishing touch for Lavender
to make. She picked a stem from her own
flower—one with a plump cluster of flowers
at its tip—and shook it near the billowing
outfits, releasing tiny spikes of lavender
laden with her own special fragrance.

Somehow, Lavender
had drifted off to
sleep. She creaked open
her tired eyelids and
sat upright on the mossy
hillock. It was still Friday.

She looked to make sure that the
party outfits were still there. They were. She
glanced at the dandelion clock nearby. Its
huge downy head was still half-full of floaty
seeds, which meant that there was plenty of
time before she had to gather and fold the
clothes for tomorrow's party.

Like a jack-in-the-box, Lavender sprang
to her feet. Then, she cupped her hands
around her mouth and bellowed loudly, in
a most unfairylike way. "Lavender's blue,
diddle diddle!"

They were strange words indeed for a
Flower Fairy who'd always considered her

flower to be lilac, mauve, or—when the sun had set—deepest purple, but according to ancient fairy tradition, this color had always been known as "blue". And it didn't really matter to Lavender, because she knew that whatever color anyone thought it was, her flower would always smell as sweet.

Chapter Two
Time for Fairy Fun!

In a flash, a cloud of bees swarmed toward
Lavender. Distracted for a moment by
the party clothes, they wove in and out of
the gossamer washing lines, nuzzling the
fragrant petals. "Bzzzzzz…" they said
approvingly.

Hot on their heels were the butterflies,
who alighted playfully on Lavender's
shoulders, whispering secrets of the world
beyond the Flower Fairy Garden to her.

A dandelion seed floated past Lavender's nose, reminding her that time was passing and spurring her into action. "Let's play a game!" she said to her hovering, dancing audience. "Hide-and-seek?"

The bees hummed happily, while the butterflies flapped their wings in agreement.

"So who'll be…?" Lavender realized that she was speaking to thin air—"it," she finished. "Looks like it'll be me, then." But, like all the other Flower Fairies in the garden, she was an obliging creature, who so loved to take part in any game that she didn't mind which part she played. She ran lightly toward the nearest flower bed, fluttering into the air with excitement every few steps.

Spotting that the snapdragons were trembling suspiciously, she crept closer and peered inside. Sure enough, the bees had

dived into the cushiony
yellow blossoms, where
they were busy sampling
the delicious nectar.

"You're it!" sang
Lavender.

There was a single lazy
buzz by way of reply, and
it dawned on her that hide-
and-seek might not be the
best game to play with a
swarm of thirsty bees...

When it was Lavender's turn to hide, she knew just the place—among the petals of her very own flower! With her lovely lilac dress she would blend right in, and surely no one would dream that she'd hide here. It was just too obvious!

So she shook her wings, took a deep breath, and—with a sparkling burst of Flower Fairy magic—flew right to the tallest stems of lavender. And she might be hiding there still, if a troublesome leaf hadn't tickled her nose.

'Aaa … Aaa … Achoo!' she sneezed, and was discovered immediately by a passing butterfly.

The butterflies had thought of an extra-clever hiding place. They darted past the white narcissus, ignoring wild bindweed in the nearby hedge, and pretended to be pretty white dresses dancing on the washing line!

"Be careful!" warned Lavender, who had been keeping a nervous eye on her precious laundry. But the butterflies told her not to worry. They knew just how long it had taken her to make everything so clean, and they weren't going to spoil it.

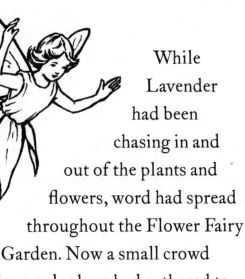

While
Lavender
had been
chasing in and
out of the plants and
flowers, word had spread
throughout the Flower Fairy
Garden. Now a small crowd
of curious onlookers had gathered to
watch the merriment.

"Hello, Lavender!" called Periwinkle, a
flaxen-haired fairy dressed in a dusky blue
tunic and sage green leggings. "Room for
one more?"

"Of course!" puffed Lavender, leaning
against a sturdy geranium stalk to catch her
breath.

"May I?" added Fuchsia. At Lavender's
nod, she performed a neat pirouette,
sending her pink and purple

petticoats spinning
outwards.

"And me?" Zinnia—who
was always brimming with
energy—flapped her beautiful
butterfly wings and fluttered to join them.

It had to be the best morning ever. They
played tag and leapfrog. They raced one
another. Then Lavender had a brainstorm—
the Flower Fairy Garden was a ready-made
obstacle course! So they chased one another
around bushes, and leaped over streams. It
was just what everyone needed after a week
of party preparations.

"Look at me!" cried Periwinkle as he looped-the-loop around a climbing plant laden with pink and lilac flowers.

"Shhhhh!" hushed Sweet Pea from a leafy perch. She raised a finger to her lips and pointed to a cluster of flowers where baby Flower Fairy Sweet Peas were snoozing. "You'll wake the little ones!"

"Ooops!" whispered Periwinkle. "Sorry about that!" He rocketed back down to the garden, landing with a thud.

Lavender winced. "Be careful," she said. "You won't be able to dance at the Midsummer Party with a sprained ankle." She turned back to the obstacle course, spying Zinnia and Fuchsia weaving in and out of the tulips.

The ground shook.

"Periwinkle," Lavender said automatically, "whatever you're doing, be sure to take care."

"Huh?" said Periwinkle.

Lavender turned to see him sitting cross-legged on the bare earth, snacking on a ripe hazelnut. The ground shook again, louder now. Whoever or whatever was making the thudding noise, it wasn't Periwinkle. So, gathering all her courage, Lavender bravely peeped around a prickly hawthorne bush and caught her breath at what she saw…

Strolling over the lawn toward them were
two human children, so tall that they blocked
out the sun. The loud noise was the sound of
a huge black-and-white ball that they were
bouncing as they walked. Thud! Thud-thud!

Lavender shrank back into the shadows
of the hawthorne bush, accidentally pricking
herself on a spike and then muffling the
squeak of pain in case they heard her.

"Sam, what's that?" said a girl with auburn
hair, a dusting of freckles, and a heart-shaped
face. "I'm sure I saw something twinkle. Do

you think it could be a fairy…?"

Her heart sinking, Lavender patted the folds of her petal dress, realizing instantly that her precious handful of fairy dust that she kept for emergencies was gone. The girl must have spotted it shining in the grass.

"Let's go and investigate!" said the other child, a boy with ruffled blond hair. "Hurry up, Milly!"

And, curious eyes fixed firmly on the ground, they crept straight toward the bottom of the garden—and the Flower Fairies.

Chapter Three
Visitors

Lavender thought back quickly over the Flower Fairy Law that every fairy was taught as soon as they were old enough… Humans—especially children—were known to be very inquisitive creatures, who had long suspected that fairies lived in their world. But if humans knew that fairies really did exist, right under their noses, the Flower Fairies' world would

be in danger of discovery. Which was why they must stay out of sight at all times.

It was time for a real-life game of hide-and-seek. Keeping under cover of the shadowy bushes, Lavender tiptoed over to where the other Flower Fairies were huddled beneath a large, leafy plant.

"Wait until you hear my splendid plan," said Periwinkle, who wasn't scared of anything. "Hiding under this—" he snapped off a dark green leaf— "I can smuggle all the Flower Fairies to safety, one by one." He looked proudly around the group as if expecting a round of applause.

"That really is a splendid plan," said Lavender, careful not to hurt his feelings, "but it's a little risky. The human children will be suspicious of anything and everything that moves."

"Ah, yes," said Periwinkle, nodding sensibly. "So what do you suggest?"

"We must hide," said Lavender. Quickly,

she told her fairy friends to find a hiding
place and stay there—no matter how close the
humans came. Most importantly, they must
stay absolutely still.

So the Flower Fairies stole away. No one
dared to fly, in case their gossamer wings were
spotted shining in the afternoon sunlight.

"Do you think we're close?" whispered Milly, so loudly that the Flower Fairies—who have incredible hearing—could hear her right at the bottom of the garden.

Despite her fear, Lavender chuckled to herself. If only humans realized just how much noise they made, they might guess why fairies were so hard to find.

"The fairies are listening to us now…" said Sam in a spooky voice. "They're hiding under this very bush." Without warning, he reached down toward the hawthorne branches where Lavender had hidden, and swept them aside. "Boo!" he said. Then, "Ouch!", as he found out how prickly it was.

Lavender sped away. While she'd been listening to the children, a plan had begun to form in her mind—an ingenious plan that would keep Flower Fairy Garden safe and keep the human children happy. But first, she had to talk to the bees and butterflies. She glanced over her shoulder as huge, shiny shoes stomped into view. Faster—she must go faster!

The bees had supped the nectar from the snapdragon flowers and were now buzzing lazily nearby, full after their sticky feast.

"Hi, Snapdragon!" Lavender waved to the

fairy snuggled comfortably between the blossoms. "Stay out of sight—there are humans around!" Snapdragon nodded and nestled farther into the flowery depths.

Lavender scampered quickly toward the bees, wishing for the thousandth time that she hadn't lost her fairy dust. And it took such a long time to make too…

Each Flower Fairy gathers pollen from their own flower, then grinds it between two rough stones until all that remains is a heap of tiny glittering particles—fairy dust. The precious dust can be used for all sorts of magical things—for summoning friendly insects and for distracting humans with its alluring sparkle. It can even be used to decorate flowers at Christmas time.

Luckily, the bees had seen Lavender, and they buzzed toward her when she called. The white butterflies came too—they had been visiting Lavender's own flowers nearby, fluttering merrily around the fragrant petals. Quickly, the Flower Fairy whispered her idea, before hurrying across to speak to Honeysuckle.

* * *

The children were really close now,
wriggling their way between overgrown
bushes and tripping over tree roots.
Occasionally, Sam would dart out a hand to
lift a smooth pebble or to examine an old,
crumbling garden ornament.

"We're never going to find anything,"
sighed Milly, looking wistfully at a mass of
elegant roses—unwittingly overlooking the
tiny fairy huddled beneath one of the flowers,
her soft pink dress and wings exactly the
same color as the rose itself.

Lavender too had concealed herself
among her own
flowers. And
as she peered
around the
garden, her keen
fairy eyes—so
much sharper than

human eyes
—saw that the
other Flower
Fairies had
done the same
thing, their outfits providing
the perfect camouflage to fool
curious children.

Milly and Sam thudded
closer and closer, until they
were so near that she could
almost touch them. A twig
snapped beneath Sam's foot,
as if signalling to Lavender
that this was the moment to set her plan
in motion. She nodded at Honeysuckle,
who was balanced high on his wild,
raggedy flower, swaying slightly in the
breeze. He blew his flowery horn loudly.
'Toot!

Milly frowned, almost as if she'd heard Honeysuckle's tiny signal, but a buzzing crowd of bees distracted her at once. They swarmed noisily into the air, where a host of white butterflies joined the throng, flitting and fluttering around crazily, like handkerchiefs waving in the distance.

Then, at another toot from Honeysuckle's trumpet… they were off! The bees and butterflies leaped from flower to flower,

pausing for a moment by the trickling stream, before continuing their merry Midsummer dance around the garden.

Eagerly, the children followed, not realizing that they were being led farther and farther away from the Flower Fairies' secret world.

"Fairies at the bottom of the garden?" gasped Sam as he dashed headlong through the flower beds, kicking the ball before him. "Rubbish! We must have seen these pesky insects!"

Milly said nothing. But she stopped for a moment and looked back longingly at the multicolored array of flowers that they'd left behind. Then she rushed after Sam.

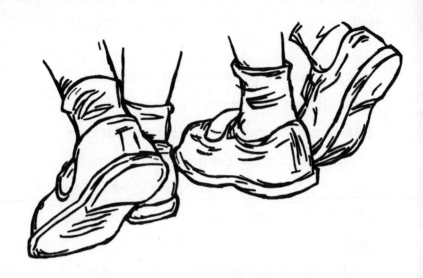

As the sound of children disappeared into the distance, an amazing transformation began to take place. The charming—if slightly overgrown—garden rustled and shook into life. Here, a dainty head peeped out of a crinkly yellow blossom. There, a tiny arm stretched from behind a stem where its owner had been hiding.

Leaves were pushed aside, petals unfolded, and long grasses moved to reveal a garden full of smiling Flower Fairies.

Lavender gazed around, thrilled that her plan had worked. But her relief turned swiftly to despair as her eyes met a dreadful sight.

She gulped, closed her eyes, and then looked again.

Oh no!

Chapter Four
Disaster!

Where the gently billowing rows of bright, clean party petals had once been, there was now only a tangled mess of gossamer and flowers.

As the children had rushed headlong after the bees and butterflies, they had snapped the delicate gossamer washing lines and trampled over the Flower Fairies' party outfits. Now all of the beautiful clothes lay on the ground, covered with mud, moss, and grass stains. Worse still, some were horribly torn.

For a moment, Lavender felt frozen to the spot. Then she sank to her knees, put her face into her hands, and sobbed.

Everything is my fault, she thought. *If only I hadn't played games earlier, I wouldn't have attracted the attention of the children… and then I wouldn't have had to dream up my stupid plan… and then the bees and the butterflies wouldn't have zoomed over the washing lines… and then the children wouldn't have stomped over the clothes.* Great fat tears slipped down her cheeks as she realized that

all of her hard work was ruined. And with no party outfits to wear, the Midsummer Party would be ruined too. If only she'd snoozed instead. If only...

Lavender listened to the cries of disappointment echoing all around. She hardly dared to look—everyone was certain to be upset and so disappointed with her. But cautiously, she lifted her head.

She needn't have worried. Everyone knew that Lavender wasn't to blame for the messy clothes. And they were such kindly creatures that they didn't blame the children either. After all, how were Milly and Sam to know that they'd been racing through a miniature laundry, when the Flower Fairies kept their world so secret?

"Don't worry," said Elder, handing Lavender a handkerchief made from her own lacy blossom.

"But everything's so d-d-dirty!" wept Lavender.

"Oh, that's not such a bad thing," said a small, exceedingly grubby little fairy, only recognizable because of the sycamore seeds he was attempting to juggle with. "If you're wearing dirty clothes, you can get up to heaps more fun!"

Sycamore's giggles were infectious,

and soon everybody was laughing—even Lavender. The Flower Fairies flocked around to comfort her, brimming with brilliant ideas and plans of action.

Periwinkle leapt on to a mushroom and cleared his throat importantly. "There's a whole day before the Midsummer Party," he announced. "That's plenty of time to get everything sorted. And we'll all lend a hand."

It was true. There was no shortage of offers to help. Flower Fairies darted here and there, collecting the clothes that had been scattered far and wide by the children's hasty feet. Carefully, Lavender examined every garment before sorting them into different piles: terribly filthy, quite dirty, slightly grubby, crumpled but clean, and absolutely spotless.

Lavender herself took charge of the "terribly filthy" pile, while advising other Flower Fairies on just the right amount of soap to use when cleaning their share of the party clothes.

There was one other sorry heap of petals —clothes that had been ripped so badly that a dunk in the stream would not fix them. And here, Tansy came to the rescue. With her tiny sewing kit—and a good helping of fairy dust—she mended rips and holes, neatened jagged edges, and replaced buttons and beads. Zinnia brought fresh petals for Tansy to patch the most ragged outfits.

Suddenly, there was an agonized shout
from the stream, and all the Flower Fairies
flung down whatever they were doing and
ran to see what was amiss. The distressed
sound was coming from Iris, who had been
allocated a pile of slightly grubby clothes
to scrub and rinse.

"What's happened now?"
wailed Lavender. Had
the children returned?
Had Iris fallen into the
river? Could today
get any worse?

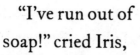
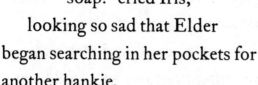

"I've run out of soap!" cried Iris, looking so sad that Elder began searching in her pockets for another hankie.

Lavender was so relieved that nothing worse was wrong, it took a moment for her to realize that this was quite a problem. Soap wasn't something that she could conjure up out of nowhere—it took time, effort, and an awful lot of ingredients.

But this time, the bees and butterflies rallied around. While Lavender searched for enough dew to fill a buttercup, they flitted here and there among the lavender flowers, collecting the petals and pollen that their Flower Fairy friend needed to make her special soap.

And so, for a second time, everything was washed and clean.

With so many creatures
helping, it was finished in
a twinkling. But things were
not destined to run smoothly in the
Flower Fairy Garden that afternoon. There
were no drying lines. Not a single one.

The spiders' delicate gossamer strands
had been snapped, tangled and ruined.
What little was left wasn't big enough to
hang a single fairy sock, never
mind an entire Midsummer
collection of clothes.
The spiders
had been
frightened

away by the
commotion and no
matter how softly
or sweetly Lavender
called, they were too
scared to return.

"If you will allow me," said
Periwinkle, bowing deeply in front of
the forlorn fairy, "I will amaze you with the
strong yet supple string I'll make from my
flower stalks, which just happen to be perfect
for washing lines. Are you watching…?"

Lavender was watching. And she was
definitely amazed.

The birds—who were quite a nosy bunch —had been watching all the frenzied fairy activity with interest. And when Rose and Honeysuckle began hanging string between the top stems of their plants, they could resist no longer. As one, they dived down to the garden to see what was going on.

"Perfect!" said Lavender, as the feathery creatures landed gracefully beside her. She'd soon realized that although Periwinkle was doing an admirable job, there was no way he could make enough washing lines to dry all the clothes before sundown.

"Here's
what I'd like
you to do," she said to the
birds.

They looked at one another curiously
and then looked back at the little Flower
Fairy, who picked a dripping-wet petal tunic
from the pile of clothes and handed it to the
first bird. "Would you fly as high as you
can and as fast as you dare until this is dry?"
Lavender asked. "Please?"

The obliging bird nodded. And soon,
the sky was fluttering with feathers and
petals. It was a beautiful sight. Lavender
paused for a moment to watch the whirl
of color, then looked down, down, down
at her checklist and heaved a great sigh.
Suddenly, the Midsummer Party seemed
as far away as ever…

* * *

If Lavender thought she'd had a busy week, it was nothing compared to her hectic Friday afternoon. She'd never had so much to do or so many people to look after. And she'd never had so much fun. Gradually, she began to forget that anything had gone wrong at all.

She masterminded the whole project, flitting here and there to make sure everything was running smoothly. Tansy was repairing torn and shredded clothes, cleverly using petals and leaves to cover the ripped edges.

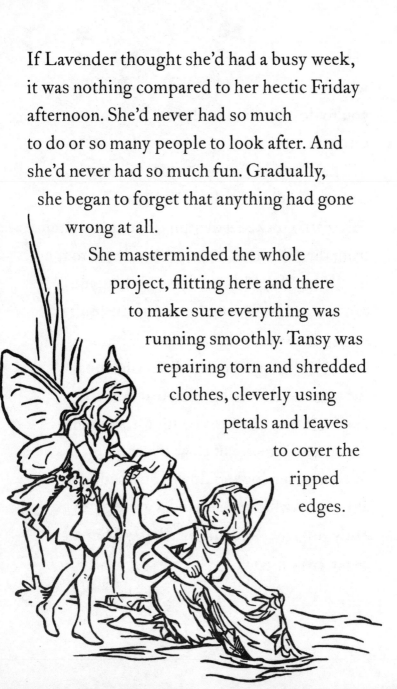

And no matter how closely Lavender looked, she was unable to spot where new petals had been sewn in place. Meanwhile, Iris was scrubbing extra hard at stubborn stains. Lavender skipped past, not forgetting to tell the hard-working fairy what a fine job she was doing, before helping to peg clean clothes on to Periwinkle's lines with bent twigs. Amongst the mayhem, she even managed to find a little time to make more fairy dust.

As the afternoon wore on, everyone began to tire.

"I'm pooped!" declared Periwinkle. He flopped down on a pillow of springy heather and mopped his brow. "I could easily go to… zzz…"

"Wake up!" said Lavender frantically. "There's still so much to do!" She tappety-tap-tapped Periwinkle's shoulder, until his eyes creaked open, but he immediately nodded off again.

"Can I help?" asked a singsong voice. It was Canterbury Bell—a blue-eyed fairy wearing a big purple hat, a pink shirt, and

shorts made from the same silvery gossamer as his wings. He held a bunch of bell-shaped purple blossoms, which he swung to and fro so that they chimed loudly.

"Me too!" added Ragged Robin, a Flower Fairy whose tattered outfit lived up to his name, and who was not often seen in these parts—his home was the wet marsh outside the garden. "I heard about the unfortunate events and came as soon as I could," he explained. "I thought a Midsummer melody might cheer everyone up." And he played a lively tune on his reed pipe.

The beautiful fairy music wafted around the garden, lifting everyone's spirits at once.

The garden was bathed in the warm, rosy glow of the setting sun as the birds dropped the last of their dry clothes into Lavender's open arms.

"Thank you!" she called as they fluttered back to their nests and perches. And tired, but happy to have helped, the Flower Fairies returned to their homes to rest before the Midsummer Party.

Tomorrow, it would be time to have fun, but now it was time to sleep. Lavender returned to her cozy bed. Most of the dainty lilac flowers were gone now, but she knew that new buds would appear soon. She laid down her sleepy head, to dream of lovely fairy friends who'd been so kind.

Chapter Five

Party Time

The next morning dawned bright and clear. Soon the Flower Fairy Garden was filled with beautiful birdsong.

It was the perfect wake-up call. Lavender opened her eyes, then stretched luxuriously. It was Midsummer's Day—the longest and most magical day of the year, and the day of the Midsummer Party. She could hardly wait!

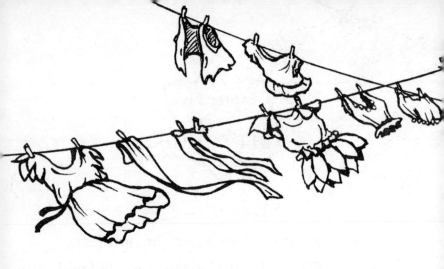

Lavender fluttered from her snuggly bed of leaves down to the green grass below and splashed her face with drops of sparkling dew.

"Now I'm ready for anything!" she announced to a passing ladybird, who flapped her spotted wings in reply.

Gathering a few last stems of Lavender from her plant and bundling them under her arm, the little lilac fairy strode purposefully toward the piles of clean party clothes and the petals still drying on Periwinkle's washing lines. For the second time that week,

she ran to and fro among the outfits, shaking
her delicate flowers all about. A gentle breeze
blew them here, there, and everywhere,
until even the air was fragrant. A musical
tinkling sound rushed through the garden,
and suddenly there was magic in the air, too,
making all the fairy petals sparkle and shine
even more than the day before.

Carefully, Lavender began to pluck
the clean clothes from the washing lines,
marvelling again at how wonderful they
looked. Soon, the pile was even taller
than her!

Lavender gently placed Elder's delicate lacy dress into her waiting arms. "Ta-daaaa!" she said proudly. There was not a mud spot to be seen.

"Oh, Lavender…" breathed the little Flower Fairy, fluttering her pale, creamy wings. "This is wonderful… However can I thank you?"

Lavender blushed as she thought of all the fairies who'd lent a hand. "I should be thanking you," she said. "Just make sure that you have a marvelous time." And, staggering slightly under her load, she hurried to meet her next satisfied customer.

"Excellent!" said Honeysuckle, admiring the extra petals that had been sewn on to the bottom of his shorts, to make them super-tough.

"Superb!" said Periwinkle, whose blue tunic had been sprinkled with fairy dust to give it a silvery sheen.

Rose was so pleased with her dainty pink frock that she was speechless.

At twelve noon precisely, Canterbury Bell's flowers began to ring merrily. It was the sound that everyone had been waiting for—the signal that the Midsummer Party was about to begin!

Dressed in their finery, the Flower Fairies skipped and danced toward a clearing in a secret corner of the garden. This was the fairy court—where the very best parties in all of Flower Fairyland took place.

Ooohs and aaahs of delight echoed through the garden as the fairies saw the mouth watering fairy feast that awaited them.

There were fairy cheeses made from Mallow's delicious seeds, piles of ripe hazelnuts, bowls of wobbly crab-apple jelly, and nutshells filled to the brim with

Elderberry's fragrant juice. The Flower Fairies piled their daisy plates high with food and dipped buttercups into the purple juice.

And then the dancing started. Honeysuckle, Canterbury Bell, and Ragged Robin provided the music, while Columbine, Almond Blossom, and Fuchsia—who needed no excuse to whirl and waltz—led the way on to the dance floor.

Lavender gazed at the dazzling jumble of color before her eyes. Everything had turned out splendidly. And everyone looked wonderful. She was having the best time!

"Excuse me?"

She looked down as a tiny Sweet Pea fairy tapped her on the knee. "Yes, my sweet?" she asked.

"I have to give you this," said the tiny fairy solemnly, handing her a scroll of fairy parchment.

Lavender's heart dropped like a stone in a very deep well. She untied the golden strands coiled around the parchment and unrolled it, her stomach turning to jelly as she did so. She gulped. The message was from the Queen of the Meadow and Kingcup. They wanted to see her—at once.

Anxious thoughts chased around Lavender's head like nervous butterflies. The king and queen must be angry with her for creating mayhem in the peaceful garden. Would they banish her from the Flower Fairy Garden…?

She went to find out.

Lavender tiptoed toward the King and Queen of the Flower Fairies, resplendent in their gorgeous royal robes. As she curtsied before them, she could not help but tremble.

"Why do you look so scared?" asked the Queen of the Meadow gently, her silky, golden hair glistening in the sunlight. She toyed with a string of olive-green pearls around her slender neck.

Lavender could not speak.

"We would like to thank you for your incredibly hard work," said Kingcup, a huge smile appearing on his handsome face. He looked around the assembled fairies, who were watching the meeting curiously. "At this time of year," he said, "Lavender becomes the most important fairy in the Flower Fairy Garden. Without her, the Midsummer Party clothes would be lackluster and dull and in some cases"—he winked at Honeysuckle—

"quite dirty. But with Lavender's efforts, everyone dazzles."

"Er… Your Kingship, sir," said Lavender, unable to stay silent. "It's thanks to all the Flower Fairies that this Midsummer Party has turned out so well this year." She curtsied apologetically.

"That is a very noble thing to say," said the Queen of the Meadow. "But even so, your contribution has been quite magnificent. And I'm sure everyone would agree."

There were deafening cheers, and Lavender blushed. She didn't think she'd ever been so proud—or so happy.

Each Midsummer Party it was traditional to reward one of the Flower Fairies by singing their special song. This year, the honor belonged, of course, to Lavender. And everyone—from the smallest Flower Fairy to the regal Kingcup—gathered round to sing:

"Lavender's blue, dilly dilly"—so goes
    the song;
All round her bush, dilly dilly, butterflies
throng;
(They love her well, dilly dilly, so do the
bees;)

While she herself, dilly dilly, sways in the breeze!

"Lavender's blue, dilly dilly, Lavender's green;
She'll scent the clothes, dilly dilly, put away clean—
Clean from the wash, dilly dilly, hanky and sheet;
Lavender's spikes, dilly dilly, make them all sweet!"

FLOWER
FAIRIES™
FRIENDS

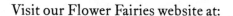

Visit our Flower Fairies website at:

www.flowerfairies.com

There are lots of fun Flower Fairy games and
activities for you to play, plus you can find out more
about all your favorite fairy friends!

Have you logged onto
the Flower Fairies™ Friends
Friendship Ring?

In the land of Fairyopolis every fairy is your friend
and now the Flower Fairies
want to share their secrets with you!

No Membership Fee

Online Fun

Visit **www.flowerfairies.com**
and sign up for the Flower
Fairies Friendship Ring
and you will receive:

- Secret Fairy Coded Messages
- News and updates
- Invitations to special events
- Every new friend receives a
  special gift from the Flower Fairies!
  (while supplies last.)

Frederick Warne & Co.
A division of Penguin Young Readers Group